T0169915

Russia and Its Islamic World

The Hoover Institution gratefully acknowledges the following individuals and foundations for their significant support of the

HERBERT AND JANE DWIGHT WORKING GROUP ON ISLAMISM AND THE INTERNATIONAL ORDER:

Herbert and Jane Dwight

Mr. and Mrs. Donald R. Beall
    Beall Family Foundation

S. D. Bechtel, Jr. Foundation

Lynde and Harry Bradley Foundation

Stephen and Susan Brown

Mr. and Mrs. Clayton W. Frye, Jr.

Lakeside Foundation

Nancy Doyle, M.D.

The Hoover Institution gratefully acknowledges
THE SARAH SCAIFE FOUNDATION
for their support of this publication.

Russia and Its Islamic World

From the Mongol Conquest to the Syrian Military Intervention

ROBERT SERVICE

HOOVER INSTITUTION PRESS

STANFORD UNIVERSITY   STANFORD, CALIFORNIA

www.hoover.org

Hoover Institution Press Publication No. 682

Hoover Institution at Leland Stanford Junior University, Stanford, California 94305-6003

First printing 2017

23 22 21 20 19 18 17   7 6 5 4 3 2 1

Manufactured in the United States of America

The paper used in this publication meets the minimum requirements of the American National Standard for Information Sciences—Permanence of Paper for Printed Library Materials, ANSI/NISO Z39.48-1992. ∞

Cataloging-in-Publication Data is available from the Library of Congress.

ISBN: 978-0-8179-2084-5 (cloth. : alk. paper)
ISBN: 978-0-8179-2086-9 (epub)
ISBN: 978-0-8179-2087-6 (mobi)
ISBN: 978-0-8179-2088-3 (PDF)

CONTENTS

ACKNOWLEDGMENTS

The idea for the book came from Charles Hill, and I am grateful for his enthusiasm and encouragement. My thanks go to Roy Allison, Jonathan Aves, Paul Chaisty, Peter Duncan, Bobo Lo, Norman Naimark, Matthew Procter, Donald Rayfield, and Harun Yilmaz for their advice on background literature. My wife, Adele, examined the draft, and her suggestions resulted in many essential changes. Jonathan Aves and Harun Yilmaz also read it through. I appreciate their suggestions for amendments and insertions—I first knew Jonathan and Harun as postgraduates, and it has been a pleasure to receive the benefit of their professional expertise. I am equally indebted to my Hoover colleague Michael Bernstam, especially for his thoughts and recollections about the 1990s. My St. Antony's colleagues Roy Allison and Eugene Rogan kindly offered helpful and incisive comments on the final draft.

Russia has long played an influential part in its world of Islam, and not all the dimensions are as widely understood as they ought to be. A vivid memory stays with me from an episode in the honeymoon that Adele and I spent in summer 1975, when we arrived from Iran in eastern Afghanistan and needed a taxi in Herat. The "car" in which we traveled one sunny afternoon had the Russian sign AMBULYANTSIA painted on both sides. The driver, when asked in Russian, revealed that he had recently spent months in Moscow as an exchange student. I had the distinct feeling, albeit unprovable, that he was some kind of Soviet "sleeper." Whatever the truth was, the experience was evidence that Russia—or, rather, the Soviet Union— was not confining itself to diplomatic overtures in trying to spread its influence to Muslim-inhabited lands thousands of miles from

Moscow. Like a lot of Sovietologists, I had taken little account of the Islamic factors in the Kremlin's politics. It was a lesson on the need to examine what happened behind the scenes of Soviet public affairs.

The Russian Federation has inherited a legacy of challenging contacts and tensions with its Islamic world. It also confronts new difficulties and opportunities. This is a volatile situation. There has never been a time when it has been more important to keep watch over how Russia, its Muslim citizens, the nearby Muslim states, and the Middle East interact with each other.

—Robert Service
April 2017

1

Russia's Long Interaction with Islam

THE RUSSIAN ENCOUNTER WITH ISLAM WAS CLOSE and problematic long before the twenty-first century. Eight hundred years earlier, Russians as a people fell under the dominion of foreign Muslim rulers. Nowadays the Kremlin dominates Muslims in the Russian Federation, exerts a deep influence upon the Muslim-inhabited states on its southern frontiers, and has lunged militarily and politically into the Middle East.

The current moment in global affairs is dangerous for Russians and the rest of us. Since the turn of our millennium, Moscow has pursued a militant agenda in its internal and external policies. Foreigners have been taken aback by the transformation, having become accustomed to a Russia that came to the West as a needy supplicant. Russia has confirmed itself as a great power even if it is no longer the superpower of yesteryear. The pacification of Chechnya and the

Syrian military intervention are the troubling examples of recent Russian assertiveness. But Russia is also entangled with its Islamic world in ways that have nothing to do with war. Muslims have for several centuries lived alongside Russians as objects of wonder and fear, and large Muslim communities continue to exist across the Russian Federation. Since the collapse of the USSR in late 1991, Russia has had to deal with the newly independent, Muslim-inhabited states on its southern frontiers. Moreover, it has chosen to interfere in Muslim states of the Middle East, building alliances and making enemies. Some features of the present-day scene display continuities with the past while others are starkly different—starkly and hazardously different.

The first impact of Muslim states on the Russian people was registered in the thirteenth century when the Golden Horde, one of the powers that emerged from the struggles inside the Mongol elite upon the death of Genghis Khan, converted to Islam. The Golden Horde for a brief while controlled all the lands from Siberia across to the Danube. The experience for Russians was lengthy and extremely brutal. The Mongols were warrior horsemen who had swept across Asia without facing effective resistance. In the course of their campaigns they adopted the Islamic faith. Islam had already spread much earlier to some of the territories of what later came to constitute Russia, including well-established communities of believers along the river Volga as well as in Siberia, the Caucasus, and the oases of Central Asia. Strapped pitilessly to the "Mongol yoke," Muscovy's Christians had to render an annual tribute to their masters from the east. The Mongol khanate all too often fixed the burden without regard for its devastating economic consequences. The Mongols executed Russian rulers and sacked their cities whenever they fell short in meeting Mongol demands.

Nevertheless, the Mongols and their allies were pragmatic enough to practice religious tolerance despite the general lacerations of their rule. As a result, the Orthodox Church survived intact two centuries of Mongol domination. Christianity provided Russians with spiritual solace and dignity and became an integral feature of their national identity. It was only a matter of time before they mounted an effective challenge to the Mongols. When in the fifteenth century the Grand Duke of Moscow, Ivan III, declared a war of liberation, he sallied forth as a Christian warrior. This time the Muscovite armies dislodged the military balance and shattered the yoke that had lain on their people's shoulders. The war had a religious dimension, since Russians were fighting as Christians against infidels. No quarter was given to the enemy by either side. Mosques were burned to the ground in celebration of the Christian triumph. The Volga region was annexed to Muscovy, and Kazan's Muslim leaders were compelled to swear fealty, just as Muscovite grand dukes had prostrated themselves in the presence of the Mongol khan. Muscovy steadily expanded its sovereignty over other areas where the Russian tongue—or something like it—was spoken. Russia was on the way to becoming one of Europe's great powers.

The fighting near the Volga was by no means over. In 1552, Ivan IV—known to history as Ivan the Terrible—laid siege to Kazan to suppress a Muslim rebellion. When Russian forces broke into the fortress, they razed the great mosque to the ground. Sultan Suleiman the Magnificent sent a message of protest from the Sublime Porte. This was an early example of the intersection of internal and external factors in Russia's Islamic world. As it happened, the Russian authorities recognized that a forcible attempt to convert Muslim communities to Christianity would be counterproductive. Muscovite interests therefore lay in granting legal status to Islam, and the Russians treated Muslims as unfortunates who persisted in the worship of a false god. (This was the mirror image of the attitude that Muslim rulers had shown to their Russian subjects.) Russians permitted the Muslim elites to stay in charge of their localities, albeit under ultimate Russian supervision and on condition that they guaranteed order and fulfilled their tax obligations. Muslim communities had no choice but to adapt themselves to Russia's legislation. But they strove to preserve what they could of sharia (Islamic law), and the Russian rulers accepted a degree of compromise as a practical necessity: Russia was vast and growing vaster, and imperial control was impossible without a degree of local acquiescence.

Russian territorial expansion continued northward toward the Baltic coast, westward across Ukraine, and eastward into the Siberian taiga and tundra. But there was no further conquest of Muslim-held territory until Russia defeated the Ottomans in the war of 1768–74 and forced them to disclaim sovereignty over the Black Sea's northern coastline. Rivalry with the Ottoman Empire had been intense ever since the Ottoman seizure of Constantinople in 1453 and the definitive destruction of the Byzantine Empire. Russia's rulers championed the peoples of Orthodox Christianity when military conditions were propitious. Ambitions of conquest, trade, and faith were intertwined. Catherine the Great's lover and general, Grigori Potëmkin, swept down into the Tatar principality of Crimea. The Tatars, or Tartars as they were usually called in Europe, had until then frustrated Russia's ambitions in regard to the Black Sea. Their involvement in the slave trade served to perpetuate the image of Islam as an alien, barbarous, and threatening phenomenon, and the jubilant Russians celebrated their Crimean success as proof of European, Orthodox Christian Russia's superiority over the rival powers of the East.

Wealthy Tatars were expelled from Crimea, provoking a growing emigration to Turkey. The tsars in subsequent decades were to contrast Crimea's Muslims with the less fiery Islamic communities of the Volga towns and villages, where Russian administrators had built up a relationship of mutual understanding in the course of two centuries of rule.

Even so, there was always a danger of Muslim revolts elsewhere in the Russian domains, which was why Catherine the Great introduced the institution that came to be known as the Orenburg

Mohammedan Spiritual Assembly, where Muslim notables gathered for discussions under official Russian supervision. The notables addressed matters pertaining to their religious and social traditions on condition that they steered clear of infringing Russia's state interests. For Russia's rulers in their capital of St. Petersburg, the Orenburg Assembly provided a means of controlling the growing number of Muslim communities. Imams could preach without interference so long as they avoided criticism of imperial authority. The central government assumed that religious devotion, education, and worship were conducive to social stability. The objective was obedience rather than conversion (although some pressure was put on Volga Tatars to declare formally in favor of Christianity). Of all the great powers apart from the Ottoman Empire, the Russians were sensitive to the possibility that disgruntled Islamic believers might rise in rebellion against their rulers and that an extreme variant of the faith might supply the motivation.

The Russian Empire raced to accumulate additional territories in the nineteenth century when yet more Muslims were brought under Russian rule. Muslim peoples in the south Caucasus—most notably the Azeris living on the eastern side of the Caspian Sea who belonged to the Shia branch of Islam—were subjugated after a long war with Persia in 1804–13. The expansionary process was resumed in later decades when vast tracts of central Asia with mainly Sunni inhabitants were subjugated. Russian power was restlessly on the march.

All this was watched with concern by Western politicians, who knew that the Russians felt frustrated by the Ottomans' continued control over the western exit of the Black Sea. Limitations remained upon Russian commercial and military access to Mediterranean waters. To many foreigners it appeared that the Russians were eyeing the Turkish-occupied parts of Europe for eventual conquest; it was assumed that the tsar's armies might also pounce on Turkey itself and subjugate the entire Middle East. Although a few Russian statesmen indeed had ambitions in this direction, they had their own worries about Ottoman pretensions. Russia found itself competing with the Ottomans for the loyalty of its Muslim subjects. The Ottoman Empire, despite weakening as an international power, retained the confidence to urge Russia's Muslims to shake off the tsarist yoke. The sultan not only wielded temporal authority but also, as caliph, was the spiritual leader of the entire Islamic world and could foment rebellion on religious principles. The tsars and their ministers had to handle their Muslim subjects with additional caution if they wanted to avoid provoking a jihad in the southernmost swaths of their empire.

Meanwhile, the tsars began to present themselves as the protectors of Christian shrines in the Holy Land regardless of the Ottoman imperial prerogatives. The Ottomans had for centuries caused trouble for the governance of the Russian Empire. Now the boot was on the other foot after the Russians became the stronger power. St. Petersburg's growing diplomatic pressure on the sultan caused agitation in London and Paris, leading in 1853 to a punitive military expedition to Crimea. Britain and France resolved to prevent the Middle East from falling into Russia's hands. The Russian armed forces, poorly organized and equipped, performed so inadequately against the Anglo-French landings that Tsar Alexander II was compelled to recognize the sovereignty of the Ottomans over their lands as the price of peace.

Russia's armies had unfinished business in the north Caucasus where Imam Shamil led an uprising in the 1830s, proclaiming a jihad against foreign military occupation. Not until 1859, after years of conflict in the mountains in and around Dagestan, was Shamil defeated and taken captive. Shamil was given dignified treatment as a way of assuring his followers that the Russians aimed to bring stability and prosperity to the region. This objective was thwarted by a revolt of the Circassians, which was finally suppressed only in 1862. The imperial authorities deported hundreds of thousands across the Black Sea to Turkey; a large number of them perished in the harsh conditions of transit. A lesson was given that if a Muslim group gave trouble, the Russian authorities would have no scruples about "cleansing" it from their territories. Expansion continued on the eastern side of the Caspian Sea, where the Turkmen people put up a bitter resistance until their defeat at the siege of Geok Tepe in 1881 and Transcaspia's annexation by the empire. For the rest of the century, the tsar's viceroy, commanders, and administrators worked to cast a net of irresistible authority over the entire Caucasus, north and south. In St. Petersburg, the desire burned as strongly as ever to wrest control of the Black Sea from the Ottomans.

Russian power penetrated deep into central Asia in the same decades. The lands of the Kazakhs, Kyrgyz, and Uzbeks were gathered into a single vast territorial unit that the Russians called Turkestan. Thus were yet more Muslims subdued. Significantly, this process brought the Russian and British colonial territories close to each other for the first time. Only Afghanistan separated the Russian Empire from British India. The Anglo-Russian rivalry became known as the Great Game, with the two sides using spies and army agents to undermine each other. The British perceived a threat to their hold on the Indian subcontinent. In Turkestan, meanwhile, Russia set about filling the sparsely inhabited steppes with Russian farmers and taming a Kazakh rebellion that lasted until 1846. A Russian governor-generalship was formally established in Tashkent in 1867 and the imperial administration was consolidated. As usual, local governance was devolved to traditional elites on condition of their political obedience. Russian culture was propagated as superior and beneficial. Alexander II's foreign affairs minister, Alexander Gorchakov, sharing the conventional European attitude of the day, referred to the process as Russia's *mission civilisatrice*.

In 1876, as the Ottomans faced growing resistance in their Balkan territories, Alexander II started a military campaign to take Istanbul (or Constantinople, as the Russians still called it) with the aim of controlling the marine exit from the Black Sea. Sultan Abdul Hamid took the banner of the Prophet Muhammad, which was in Ottoman safekeeping, and declared a jihad against the invaders. But Russian imperial forces reached the outskirts of Istanbul by the start of 1878, forcing Abdul Hamid to accept an armistice. At the Congress of Berlin later that year, the Ottomans lost two-fifths of their empire, including three provinces in eastern Anatolia which were given to the Russians—and yet more Muslims thereby became subjects of the tsar.

According to the 1897 Russian census, nearly fourteen million people professed the Islamic faith, which was 11 percent of the empire's population. Most of the Muslim subjects of the tsars gave them little cause for concern. But the Caucasus and central Asia remained pinch points of governance in a period when Russia wanted to assert itself against the rival powers on its borders. The Caucasian territories provided Russia with its second biggest Muslim area and population after the Volga region. The Kabardinians and Ossetians were swiftly pacified, and their leaders were granted titles of Russian nobility. Christian Georgia, too, had its aristocracy incorporated in the Russian social ranking. But the tsars declined to accord aristocratic status to the Muslim elites in Azerbaijan. The Azeris, as it happened, were obedient to Russian rule. But Chechen Muslims on the northern slopes of the Caucasus proved more resistant, and the Chechen territory seethed with discontent. Conquest, difficult though it had been, was easier than administrative control. The maintenance of power in the north Caucasus alone devoured a quarter of the annual state budget. Ministers could never afford to overlook the mood of its millions of Islamic believers. Empire was a costly asset.

Discontent with the political and social system was reaching the boil by the turn of the century, and in 1905–06 a revolutionary emergency enveloped Nicholas II and his government. While workers, peasants, and sections of the middle class in Russia jointly challenged the authoritarian order in society, disturbances broke out in the north Caucasus. Dagestan and neighboring Chechnya were hot spots of rebellion. Muslims elsewhere, too, demanded fundamental reforms or joined in outright rebellion. Nicholas agreed to hold elections to a parliamentary assembly known as the State Duma; at the same time he ordered a severe repression of revolutionary organizations. He survived in power, but the assertive spirit persisted throughout society. The Tatars of the Volga region, for instance, petitioned to be recognized as Muslims rather than as the Christian converts that had previously been the status of many of them; they wanted to free themselves from sin by obtaining an end to the restrictions on sharia law. With the monarchy and the Orthodox Church on the defensive, the habits of compromise suddenly seemed unnecessary and even indecent. But Nicholas II succeeded in facing down such challenges. Although his administration incurred endless criticism in the new parliament, he restored most aspects of his authority over policy.

When the Great War broke out in 1914, Tsar Nicholas obtained the agreement of his French and British allies to Russia's old objective of annexing Istanbul and monopolizing control of the Black Sea. The tsar's conservative and liberal critics shared this goal but objected to his refusal to allow the formation of a government accountable to the State Duma. The ensuing wartime travails disrupted the civilian economy and undermined social amenities as priority was given to the armed forces, and blame was increasingly heaped upon Nicholas. Strikes broke out in Russian industrial cities in 1915–16.

The Ottomans entered the war on the side of Germany and Austria-Hungary. Among Sultan Mehmed V's first steps was his declaration of a jihad against Britain, France, and Russia, whose empires ruled well over half of the world's Muslims. The Germans hoped that Mehmed's words would persuade Muslim communities to rise in revolt and cause a serious disruption of the Allied war effort. In fact, the Russian Empire experienced little disturbance in its Muslim-inhabited territories until 1916, when ministers responded to the growing labor shortage by conscripting half a million young

Muslim men to serve in work units behind the front lines. Immediately mullahs told everyone that the recruits would be sent against fellow Muslims: the Ottoman armies. This restoked the fires of revolt in central Asia as Muslim militants attacked Russian settlers, garrison soldiers, and even Islamic dignitaries. Ninety thousand or more rebels were killed in the operation to pacify the region. It was a bloody example of the intersection of internal and external factors in Russia's treatment of its Muslim subjects.

It was also the most serious uprising in the empire at war until March 1917, when political demonstrations of workers and garrison troops overwhelmed the authorities in the Russian capital, now renamed Petrograd. After learning that the general staff shared the judgment of conservative and liberal political leaders that there was no prospect of restoring order while he stayed on the throne, Nicholas II felt compelled to abdicate. The liberal-led Provisional Government took office, but it proved unable to prevent the collapse of the economy and administrative order; workers' and soldiers' councils (or soviets) came under the sway of Vladimir Lenin and his communist party. In October, the communists seized power and established a Soviet dictatorship, proclaiming the goal of spreading communism around the world. Muslims, like every other social and religious group, had already taken the opportunity of revolutionary times to demand better treatment from the government regardless of who headed it. The outlying regions seceded from Russia either because of chronic hostility to Russian control or in rejection of the communism that Lenin was striving to impose. Scores of regional wars broke out. The peoples of central Asia and the north Caucasus were prominent in declaring their independence, and jihadists were among the militant forces.

But the Red Army had superior weaponry and organization. Once it had achieved mastery in Russia, the borderlands were easy prey for it. The communist administration was two-faced in the way that it handled national and religious organizations. Its armed forces frequently acted as if they were traditional imperialists in Red disguise, and military atrocities were widely attested. What is more, the Reds were militant atheists who were just as likely to burn down mosques and execute mullahs as they did churches and priests in Russia. In the peace that followed, however, Lenin insisted on allowing Muslims to practice their faith as they liked in those parts of the country where they were in the majority. Communists were confident that they could win the struggle for Muslim sympathy and appealed to young Muslim men and women to rally to the Soviet cause. Trainee mullahs were welcomed into the communist party so long as they opposed the conservative features of contemporary Islamic society. The aim was to foster an acceptance of Marxism by persuasion and education and then to use the Tatar, Azeri, Uzbek, and Dagestani youngsters to propagate communist doctrines in their native cities and villages. The communists were indulging religion only as a prelude to bringing all religious belief to an end.

Lenin and his fellow party leaders Leon Trotsky and Joseph Stalin calculated that the cause of world revolution would benefit if the word spread that Muslims were treated better under communism than in the Muslim lands colonized by the European overseas empires. In 1920 a conference was organized in Azerbaijan for "the peoples of the East," welcoming many delegates who endorsed the communist "anti-imperialist" agenda while continuing to profess their own Islamic faith. Azerbaijan, with its Muslim population, was the new Soviet socialist republic created after the Red Army overthrew the independent state that had been formed two years earlier. The Soviet leadership in Moscow gave advancement to political recruits who had been brought up as Muslims; and although such individuals were few in number, they served as exemplars of communism's capacity to bring education and economic progress to countries held back by imperial dominance and culturally reactionary imams. Communists presented themselves as the enablers of enlightenment.

Their aim was to subvert the European empires by establishing communist parties and spreading anti-imperialist propaganda around the world. The Middle East, where the British and French secured protectorates after the First World War, was a prime target. Funds were released to send agents to conduct agitation throughout the region. But the Kremlin leaders were also acutely aware of the threats to their own power that could spill out of the Middle East. As the Ottoman Empire fell apart at the end of the war, Moscow had grounds for concern about the various armed forces that were being formed in Turkey. Enver Pasha led his hastily assembled Army of Islam into Azerbaijan in 1918, forcing Christian Armenian inhabitants to flee for their lives—Enver was already notorious as one of the wartime architects of the genocidal policy toward the Armenians in the Ottoman lands. In 1921, Soviet Russia, smarting from the invading Red Army's defeat in Poland, signed treaties with the Turks as well as with the Afghans and Iranians with a view toward securing its southern territories in what was about to be designated as the Union of Soviet Socialist Republics.

The new Turkish government under Mustafa Kemal pursued secularist policies and in 1924 abolished the caliphate. Kemal, furthermore, distrusted Enver and his Islamist inclinations. Enver's ultimate aim had been to unite Turkey with most of the peoples of the Caucasus and central Asia through an ideology that became known as pan-Turkism. To Kemal this was further proof that Enver was a rival commander whose utopian schemes could endanger Turkey's security.

Nevertheless, a variant of the dream of amalgamating the Muslim-inhabited lands of the former Russian Empire was espoused by a young Volga Tatar communist called Mirsaid Sultan-Galiev. At first the Politburo had welcomed the educated and talented Sultan-Galiev as exactly the kind of party recruit who would help to spread Soviet power in the southern borderlands. But his calls for religious and territorial autonomy started to horrify the Politburo—so much so that Sultan-Galiev was arrested in 1923 on the charge of having betrayed the communist party's goal of unifying the multinational state and moving toward the elimination of religion. Despite being released, he was put in prison again in 1928 and executed in 1940. The Kremlin was determined to ensure that the Muslims of the USSR would drop any lingering dream of a future in which Moscow would no longer exercise direct control.

Until nearly the end of the 1920s, nevertheless, the Politburo made energetic efforts to appeal to the country's Muslims. Recognizing how very few Azeris were communists, it absorbed the left wing of Azerbaijan's Himmät (Endeavor) socialist party into the new Communist Party of Azerbaijan. Lenin had set an agenda for large regions to gain the status of Soviet republics within a USSR. Among other things, this was a way of dividing up the Muslims and preventing any attempt to unite them on the basis of Islam. Instead, the communist agenda offered autonomy to national territories inside a formal federal structure. The Politburo hoped that this would rob nationalism of its vigor and lay the groundwork for the various peoples to trust the communist leaders and welcome communist doctrines as their guiding philosophy.

The Moscow leadership had shed the illusion that religion would disappear quickly. But measures were taken to disseminate atheism in schools and in the press, and the League of the Militant Godless was founded to stage public events that ridiculed everything that the clergy of all faiths preached about God. The Politburo sustained an aggressive policy toward the Russian Orthodox Church out of fear that its bishops and priests would act as a rallying point for counterrevolutionary agitation among Russians. If the Orthodox Patriarch spoke out for Christianity and patriotism, a resurgence of anticommunist activities might destabilize the Soviet order—and the Church priesthood might triumph where the anti-Bolshevik White commanders had failed. But the communists treated most of the other Christian denominations more gently. They did this partly to sow seeds of dissension between Orthodox Christians and the so-called sects, partly out of the cynical consideration that by granting a degree of freedom to some denominations, they would secure their gratitude and compliance. It was a complex situation. Religion was being semi-tolerated at the same time as it was being undermined by political indoctrination: the struggle was joined for the hearts and minds of Soviet citizens.

The surviving mosques started to flourish in the Volga region, Azerbaijan, and central Asia. Precious ancient copies of the Koran were restored to Muslim communities. The communists funded the establishment of schools to eradicate illiteracy; education was provided in the local languages. In the case of those peoples of the north Caucasus where the culture remained an exclusively oral one, this required the creation of usable alphabets. University linguistics departments dispatched students during each summer vacation to learn the languages so as to accelerate the process. State favor was reserved for those imams who advocated economic and social modernization. Communist policies were aimed at breaking the shackles of age-old "superstition." With this in mind, the party sought to appeal especially to Muslim youth and to Muslim women. Communists campaigned strongly against the old patriarchal traditions. Fathers who refused to adapt to the new ways were derided; female Muslims of every age were urged to abandon wearing the veil and seek paid employment outside the home. Wherever possible, indigenous political leaders were appointed to lead the local administrations. Moscow's communist leadership searched out Muslim reformers—who called themselves *jadids*—to form an alliance with Soviet institutions.

2

Muslims in the Russian Cultural Imagination

RUSSIANS FOR CENTURIES HAD DEFINED THEMSELVES by reference to their national tormentors. The Mongols were the oldest enemy in folk memory, and the Orthodox Church continued to preach the gospel against Muslim unbelief. Muslims were not the only people regarded with suspicion in Russia. Wars with Poland left a lasting legacy of tension between the Russian and Polish nations, and the Catholic Poles appeared to Orthodox Russians in a poor light. When Catherine the Great, in concert with Austria and Prussia, helped to bring about the partition of Poland in the late eighteenth century, Russia acquired provinces with a large Jewish as well as Polish population. The Orthodox clergy had long treated Catholics as beneath contempt and dismissed Jews as the "tribe" of Christ-killers. Although the Russians were not alone in looking down on and fearing their neighbors, they were more than averagely xenophobic, as travelers to the country frequently noted. Thus, it was very far from being the case that the Russian nation, from the aristocracy down to the peasantry, was preoccupied by a singular unease about Muslims inside and outside the empire. Even so, anti-Islamic ideas were undoubtedly in the air that Russia's Christians breathed.

Not until the nineteenth century did Russian writers and other artists gain a degree of freedom to answer the question of what it was to be a Russian without regard to how the tsar or the church answered it. Despite tight censorship, the intelligentsia sneaked its ideas into the arena of public discussion.

The poets Alexander Pushkin and Mikhail Lermontov and the novelist Lev Tolstoy were early contributors. The three of them drew attention to the armed conflict that inflamed the entire north Caucasus as the Russian Empire imposed direct rule. Each author made heroes of the ordinary Russian conscripts who endured the hardships of military campaigns. Taken away from the huts and soil of their native villages, peasant soldiers had to adapt to the southern landscape with its cliffs, crevasses, scrubland, and dense forests. The officer corps, too, had to adapt to the kind of hit-and-run fighting that for centuries had been practiced in the mountains. Pushkin, Lermontov, and Tolstoy ridiculed the pampered, privilege-ridden culture that the Russian ruling elite on active service had to leave behind. For these writers, the wars of the Caucasus put Russians on their mettle, bringing out the best in the best of them regardless of their class background. While the St. Petersburg newspapers were duly reporting on the carnage, creative writers provided a vivid account of its effect on the rulers and the ruled. In the process, they wrote about Islam.

Pushkin had lived in the Caucasus in the course of his political exile from St. Petersburg; Lermontov and Tolstoy had been on active service in the wars of the Caucasus. Even Tolstoy, who turned pacifist in middle age, had once implied that Russia's imperial expansion was in the nature of things. None of them had originally asked himself whether Russians had the right to annex the mountain peoples and their homelands.

About these peoples, they had mixed feelings. Russian authors, like other Europeans affected by an attitude that would later be dubbed "orientalism," portrayed their "Eastern" characters as wild and ruthless. Caucasian customs appeared to them uncivilized. Most local inhabitants were impervious to Russian cultural influence long after their military defeat. Their vengefulness was notorious. They continued the practice of taking Russian women into captivity and forcing them into marriage. They seized stray Russian soldiers and held them for ransom. Their word seemed unreliable—Russians seldom paused to ask themselves why Russia's armies deserved better treatment than the peoples of the Caucasus were receiving. The classical writers highlighted the squalor of the Muslim villages and the dominance exerted by their headmen. They regarded the mountain ethnicities as being chained to age-old traditions, oblivious of the Enlightenment ideas that had penetrated the Russian upper classes in recent decades. Prose and poetry highlighted the Caucasian preference for violence over peaceful negotiation in the settlement of disputes. A mountaineer saw his best friend as his gun or dagger. By extending Russian imperial territory southward, the tsars and their generals were drawing an obscure and dangerous region under their authority.

The same writers saw something magnificent in the mountain peoples, describing them as children of nature existing almost in a state of divine grace. Unspoiled by urban living, they were depicted as being able to walk through forests without rustling a leaf. Russia's creative artists were doing the same as their counterparts to the west, who romanticized those Gallic and Germanic tribes that rejected and resisted the urban ways of the invading Romans. According to many Russian authors, the "civilization" brought by the Russians and their armies had a corrupting impact. The Caucasians might be rough-and-ready, but they kept to their own codes of honor and conduct in their dealings with each other—and they seldom infringed them. The way that they upheld their customs of family and faith impressed a generation of novelists, poets, painters, and composers who were famous for questioning everything about Russian life and human existence in general.

One of the century's most esteemed Russian painters, Vasili Vereshchagin, lived for some years in Tashkent after its conquest and produced exuberant canvases of central Asian scenes. He, too, laid stress on the exotic character of the peoples who were becoming known to the Russians. Uzbeks appear in their flowing robes and headdresses. Vereshchagin rendered the battles that led to the imperial occupation. Russian soldiers are shown in compact, disciplined formations, whereas the opposing warriors are presented as wild, unrestrained, and ferocious. Muslim urban residents in his paintings are often fanatical dervishes or sadistic tormentors of their captives, and other local characters are represented as indolent or corrupt. Vereshchagin was of the opinion that conquest was good for those who had been conquered. His brilliant photo-realist technique earned commissions from the Russian high command to produce vast canvases celebrating military victories. Over the years he came to change his attitude and began to regard the local inhabitants with sympathy. By the end of his life he was an outright opponent of violence. By then, however, he had achieved fame in the great galleries of Russia and Europe because of those early paintings that idealized the imperial army.

Tolstoy had a steadier perspective. In 1872 he published the novella *Prisoner of the Caucasus*, in which he drew movingly on his memories of active service. The central character is a Russian army officer called Zhilin who is heading home on leave to see his aged mother. As he rides through a mountainous area with his military companion Kostilin, Chechen villagers pull them off their horses and bind them with shackles before imprisoning them in one of their barns. It becomes clear that they have fallen into the hands of Abdul-Murat, who orders them to write to their families and ask for payment in return for their freedom. The two officers have become a commercial asset. Abdul-Murat sees no point in coddling his victims and puts them on a meager diet, just enough for them to subsist. Weeks pass, and Zhilin makes friends with an unmarried young girl, Dina, who takes pity on the Russians and provides them with food of better quality. Zhilin and Kostilin witness some of the village's Islamic practices as a mullah utters a prayer for a dead Muslim fighter and a mare is slaughtered for the funeral feast. It is a new world for the Russian captives.

Zhilin and Kostilin decide to attempt their escape by dead of night after they despair of gaining their freedom in any other fashion. As they scramble over the nearby hills, they lose their way and Kostilin injures his foot. Though Zhilin carries him onward for some distance, their angry pursuers catch up with them. Bound and taken back to the village, the captives provoke noisy debate. One old man shouts out: "It is a sin to feed Russians. Kill them and have done with it!" But Abdul-Murat wants his ransom money, warning Zhilin that if he tries to flee for a second time he will kill him "like a dog." Zhilin and Kostilin are then taken down in shackles into a pit that is twelve feet square. They receive only unbaked dough for food. But the girl Dina again takes pity on them and provides them with a long pole with which to climb out of the pit. Dina runs after Zhilin outside the village and helps to break off his shackles. At that very moment, horsemen can be heard in the vicinity. Zhilin fears that they are Muslim pursuers, but in fact they are fifteen Cossacks. The novella ends happily as Zhilin rejoins his regiment.

Tolstoy tried to give a fair account of Russia's Muslims. Although some of them appear as embittered brutes, even Abdul-Murat the ransom-gatherer has some decent features. If anyone is the hero of the tale, it is not Zhilin but Dina.

Literature about the north Caucasus was essentially as much about contemporary urban Russia as it was about conditions in the newly conquered mountains. Tolstoy and other outstanding nineteenth-century authors wrote little about the other newly conquered regions of the empire. Thus they all but overlooked several huge swaths of territory with large Muslim populations. No outstanding novelist or poet emulated the painter Vereshchagin and focused on central Asia. Even Crimea was only fitfully considered, as in Lermontov's evocative short tale *Taman* or Tolstoy's *Sevastopol Stories*, which were based on his Crimean War experience. Almost nothing influential was published about Azerbaijan or central Asia apart from official military and administrative reports. What is more, Islam itself was of little interest to Russian authors, and next to no notice was taken of Koranic doctrine or of the religious splits within Muslim communities. And although the literary giants provided a more nuanced analysis than the Islamophobic one that the Orthodox Church propounded, they still allowed plenty of scope for Russians to deprecate Muslims and their beliefs. Generation after generation in subsequent years were reared on a fare of dislike and distrust.

Direct engagement with the Islamic question tailed off in the early twentieth century, when Russian artistic figures ceased to pursue an interest in imperial problems. Not that they lost interest in the exotic and the "oriental." Igor Stravinsky's *Rite of Spring* explored the wild recesses of human society far from the glare of "civilization." Alexander Blok's *Scythians* was a poem of wonder about the untamed people who had once inhabited the area to the north of the Black Sea. Pushkin, Lermontov, and Tolstoy had preferred to write of observable Chechens, Ingush, and Kabardinians, whereas Stravinsky and Blok presented their themes through the prism of myth.

The October 1917 Revolution introduced an antireligious imperative to state cultural policies as the communist leaders sought to dissolve popular attachment to the Christian, Muslim, and Jewish faiths. The Islamic question fell into neglect in the 1920s and 1930s. When Alexei Tolstoy, a distant relative of the great novelist and a writer in his own right, published his best-selling *The Russian Character* in the Second World War, he saw no need to mention Muslims or religious believers of any kind. Even so, Alexei's late relation was far from being a lifeless literary relic because Stalin, Lenin's successor as communist party leader, was keen to make his selection of the Russian cultural canon available to all the citizens of the USSR. The fact that Lev Tolstoy had been a Christian and an anarchist was ignored in favor of recognizing him as an author who loved Russian people below the level of the country's ruler and clerics. The novel *War and Peace* and the novella *Prisoner of the Caucasus* were republished in vast print runs and placed on the compulsory school curriculum. Thus it came about that Marxism was taught in schools alongside nineteenth-century narratives about the great Russian past. Every student, including those who had never been to the north Caucasus, gained a feeling from the work for the mountains and their peoples.

After Stalin's death in 1953, Russian nationalism discreetly reared its head in literary prose and films after a campaign to protect the Orthodox Church's architectural heritage obtained official approval. But Islam was neglected by the Russian cultural intelligentsia until after the fall of communism in the USSR.

One of the most remarkable movies on a theme involving Muslims was *Prisoner of the Caucasus*, directed by Sergei Bodrov and released in 1996. The plot closely follows that of Tolstoy's nineteenth-century novella but is set in the last years of the twentieth century when Russians and Chechens were at war. Once again the captured Russian officer is called Zhilin and his captor's name is Abdul. Whereas the novella described its Chechen village as squalid and poverty-stricken, Bodrov stresses that it is the nearby Russian-inhabited hamlet that is dirty and full of demoralized families and individuals. Abdul, so far from being a money-grubber, is decent and dignified and sees his way to releasing Zhilin even though the Russian armed forces have murdered his son, a schoolteacher. The film has a convulsive last scene in which Zhilin walks down the slopes from the village and a Russian military helicopter squad appears in the sky above him. Although Zhilin's fate is not disclosed, the somber closing music implies unmistakably that he is in mortal danger. In Tolstoy's original novella there is no comment on the Russian government or high command. Zhilin in Bodrov's movie owes more to his Chechen captors than to any of his comrades, ministers, or commanders. A cultural debate that began with Pushkin and Lermontov retains its vitality.

The movie won the applause of discerning Russian viewers. It is easy to understand why if it is remembered how negatively Islam had been treated in the official Soviet media from the late 1920s onward. By the 1990s, this served to pique people's curiosity about the religion. Bodrov's film was one of the first public attempts by a non-Muslim since the nineteenth century to suggest that a life lived by Islamic precepts was other than backward or threatening. Those viewers who had an open mind on the subject learned respect for an alien culture, a culture that existed widely across the former Soviet Union.

3

The Communist Offensive against Islam

DECADES EARLIER, IN 1928, STALIN HAD STARTED A crash program of industrialization. Agriculture was forcibly reorganized and a system of collective farms was imposed. Political repression was intensified. Among the targets of the party's efforts were public figures who had made a name for themselves as national or religious leaders. Even many of those Muslims who had gone over to communism were persecuted. Imams were arrested and many mosques were demolished. The maltreatment was especially severe among the Muslim nomads in Kazakhstan, where the Politburo enforced the priority for cereal crop production. The savagery of Soviet collectivization was conducted behind a veil of secrecy in Ukraine, where only a handful of inquisitive Western journalists reported on the mass hunger. The parallel process in Kazakhstan totally escaped foreign attention since no reporter set foot there. Nomads were violently "sedentarized," which involved being forced to work in the new collective farms and achieve the wheat output quotas that Stalin imposed. So brutal were the methods used in this operation that half the Kazakh population starved to death within half a decade.

This was only the beginning of Stalin's assault on faith, tradition, and national self-expression in the cause of "modernity." Throughout the 1930s, Stalin attacked all forms of religion and every kind of cleric. Imams were specifically designated as "anti-Soviet elements" in the vicious program of arrests and executions that were to become known as the Great Terror of 1937–38. This happened despite the formal guarantee of universal national and religious rights in the Soviet Constitution enacted in 1936. Even those political appointees from the north Caucasus, Azerbaijan, and Kazakhstan who had avoided trouble in the late 1920s were swallowed into the maw of the mass repressions. Resistance to Russians and to communism had not ceased in central Asia after the civil war, and it persisted, often with jihadi objectives, into the mid-1930s as the so-called Basmachi maintained their revolt in Tajikistan and Kyrgyzstan. Some of the rebels found respite across the Afghan border. But the Red Army outmatched them in organization and firepower, and the ultimate triumph of the communist order was never in serious doubt.

Stalin no longer had it in mind to compromise with the non-Russian peoples but rather to subordinate them to Great Russia. It was to be a Russia that was built in his image, a Russia of gigantic factories, powerful armies, and militant atheism. Official Russian nationalism was an idiosyncratic phenomenon in the decades of Stalin's rule because it involved a rejection of the church, the village, and the peasantry. In the previous century, all the nationalists had eulogized these three as being the foundations of the Russian people's greatness. Now rural traditions were to be eradicated, and the sooner the better. Stalin's new Soviet Russia was paraded as the engine of communist progress. The USSR's status as the heir to the empire of the tsars was extolled. Although most tsars continued to be anathematized, those who extended the frontiers by conquest received some official approval. The latter included pitiless rulers such as Ivan the Terrible and Peter the Great. But whereas the tsars and their generals had been cruel during wars of conquest, Stalin carried out his atrocities in peacetime. He praised the Russian nation as "the elder brother" of all the Soviet peoples; school textbooks, including those written for specific nations in republics outside Russia, highlighted the benefits of belonging to a multinational state based upon the achievements of modern Russian culture.

Past leaders of resistance to Russian imperial expansion were written off as ignorant and deluded. Whereas under Lenin they had been renowned as anti-tsarist militants, under Stalin they were made to appear as troublemakers who had applied the brakes to the chances of progress on offer to the unenlightened masses in the outlying lands. This signaled a reversion to attitudes that had prevailed under the tsars. The difference was that before the collapse of the Romanov monarchy, Russians had been enjoined to stand fast by their Orthodox Christian beliefs and look down on Islam as an inferior faith, misguided at best and menacing at worst. (It ought to be added that teachers in madrasas and mosques had dismissed Christians as the ignorant godless.) Stalin did away with such niceties. He wanted to remodel Great Russia's nationhood according to the precepts of Marxism-Leninism, so Islam in the USSR fell victim alongside Christianity and Judaism to his fanaticism. The state economic plans contained no budget to build mosques or madrasas. On the contrary, the government was turning centers of Islamic devotion into warehouses. In 1917 there were 24,582 registered mosques; fewer than 4,000 survived by the end of the 1920s. Only 416 remained by the late 1940s.

The Soviet regime treated the followers of the Koran with deliberate harshness. In new cities and old, the cafeterias sold meals without regard to halal requirements. If Muslims wanted to eat, they had to accept what everyone else was getting. Similarly, devout Jews had no public access to kosher food, and Christians could not buy traditional fare at Christmas or Easter.

After Hitler invaded the USSR in 1941, Stalin pragmatically adjusted policy by lessening his persecution of religion in the interests of widening popular support for the war effort. Although the Russian Orthodox Church was the main beneficiary, Stalin renewed the official recognition of Islam by establishing Muslim spiritual directorates. But he also designated certain entire "nationalities" as enemy peoples. Discrimination against ethnic Germans might have been expected, but it came as a devastating surprise when Stalin's security forces began an operation to deport all Chechens, Ingush, Crimean Tatars, and Kalmyks from their ancestral homelands into the wilds of Kazakhstan. The Chechens, Ingush, and Crimean Tatars were mostly of the Islamic faith. Vast numbers of them died in the savage course of deportation. Stalin was punishing them for collaborating with the German occupation. He ignored the fact that thousands of them had fought in the Red Army and many had won military decorations for valor. The result was to sharpen the ill feelings about Russian power that lasted through to the death of Stalin in 1953 and beyond.

Stalin's successor, Nikita Khrushchëv, allowed the deported peoples to return from Kazakhstan (except for the Crimean Tatars, whose homeland was regarded as of overriding strategic importance). But he remained utterly intolerant of their religious observances. Khrushchëv, an antireligious zealot, knocked down many of the places of worship that even Stalin had left standing. Mosques were demolished along with churches and synagogues, and the secret police, now called the KGB, arrested many imams and mullahs. A watch was kept on Friday sermons at the few remaining registered places of Muslim worship. The consequence was that Islam was driven more deeply underground throughout the USSR. Muslims concluded that they would never receive an honored place in public affairs or social life under the Soviet communist order.

The campaign against religion was somewhat wound down in 1964 when the central political leadership replaced Khrushchëv with his protégé Leonid Brezhnev, who allayed worries among officials that he might fire a large number of them as Khrushchëv had been wont to do. Instead he announced a policy of "stability of cadres," which meant that politicians had a guaranteed job for life. Although this helped Brezhnev secure his position as the communist party leader, over time it had the predictable effect of strengthening the networks of political patronage below the heights of the Politburo. Nowhere was the problem more acute than in central Asia and the north Caucasus, where local leaders, building on age-old social practices, gave preferment to members of their own clans or extended families. Ancient customs that had been laid aside or suppressed were quietly restored. Although the Russian language was necessarily used in administrative documents, the inhabitants of the "Muslim" Soviet republics increasingly used the native languages among themselves and resisted pressures to give influential jobs to Russians. A silent process of decentralization and "nationalization" of day-to-day authority occurred.

Dinmukhammed Kunaev, the first secretary of the Kazakhstan communist party, was promoted to full Politburo membership. Republics such as Kazakhstan, Uzbekistan, and Tajikistan were left alone so long as they met the output targets of the five-year economic plan and paraded their dedication to Brezhnev and his policies. Central Asian communists were notorious for their fawning affirmations of devotion to Moscow's interests. This masked a reality of gross republican delinquency. Although cases of financial corruption occasionally came to light, Brezhnev forbore to undertake a systematic project of firings or judicial proceedings. In Uzbekistan the communist party first secretary, Sharif Rashidov, oversaw the development of an entire illegal parallel economy. He and his officials supplied two-thirds of the Politburo's cotton harvest requirements while engaging in a secret trade, including exports, in the annual surplus crop. Palatial private residences were built by Rashidov's cronies. Even an underground jail was constructed to hold those Uzbeks who threatened to expose what was happening. Communist authoritarianism was locally applied to maintain the status quo, and a whole generation of young people were brought up to assume that graft and fraud were integral and desirable cogs in the workings of the economic order.

It is true that the Politburo could point to advances in health care and education in Soviet central Asia. Transport and several economic sectors had been modernized since the 1930s. Compared to Afghanistan and regions of other countries across the USSR's southern frontier, Kazakhstan and Uzbekistan had achieved considerable social progress; and there was a grudging recognition of this in the outlying republics, among many members of the educated classes.

But when Brezhnev died in 1982, the lid was prized open to reveal the scale of corruption as well as the spread of Islam. The Politburo found itself considering reports that Islamic practices, so far from fading in the old Muslim areas of the USSR, were attracting a growing number of adherents. Even individuals who did not attend mosques or have personal access to a Koran were likely to comply with Muslim tenets on family life and the status of women—and some of the more fervent believers urged family and friends to prevent their young men from being conscripted into the Soviet armed forces. By reducing the number of registered mosques, moreover, the communist administration involuntarily prepared the ground for the influence of unofficial religious leaders. Islam relies to a lesser extent on official buildings for worship than many Christian denominations. The consequence was that believers congregated in sport clubs, bakeries, or even warehouses to hear prayers and sermons. Marxism had set down few healthy roots in Muslim society, and the regrowth of religious commitment was widely noted. Decades of atheistic propaganda had fallen on barren soil.

The evidence was unmistakable. Circumcision of young boys was a widespread rite in central Asia and parts of the north and south Caucasus. Pork was avoided. Girls were married earlier than was usual in the rest of the USSR. There were readings of the Koran at weddings and funerals—and even officials of party and government complied with Muslim traditions of marriage, funerals, circumcision, and fasting. They knew that they were otherwise likely to lose the respect of the local population.

Although the KGB provided alarming analyses of such phenomena, the Politburo had too many other concerns on its agenda—Afghanistan, Poland, economic decline, and the arms race with the United States—to give priority to questions of Islam in the USSR. In any case, the survival of a large Muslim element in the general population had always been a source of bafflement for Kremlin politicians. Why, they asked, did Islam retain so vibrant an appeal after decades when atheist ideas were taught to schoolchildren? Communist leaders throughout the Soviet Union had been brought up to revere the philosophical notion that God does not exist. For them, atheism was axiomatic, and religion was the opium of the people. The result was that they could frame many questions about Islam but were incapable of answering them. The Islamic faith grew ever stronger in its traditional territories. Muslim societies organized secret meetings for prayer and religious education, while bright young devotees were subsidized to make illegal trips to Mecca and Cairo, where they could train as imams before returning home. Although religious faith was not the main solvent of the political order in the USSR as a whole, it was an important element in the gradual process of dissolution, at least in the Muslim-inhabited republics.

4

The Soviet Quest
Abroad for
Muslim Allies

ONE OF THE CONTRADICTIONS OF THE POSTWAR SITU-
ation was the fact that while the communists continued their
campaigns to eradicate religion from the USSR, they made overtures
in foreign policy to countries in what was called the Third World,
many of which had large Muslim majorities. Khrushchëv had introduced this approach as part of his effort to challenge America's global
influence. Funds were reserved for military and economic assistance to governments that were willing to detach themselves from
the American embrace. In the Middle East, Turkey and Iran were
already among Washington's firm allies, so Soviet leaders had to look
elsewhere for friends. Khrushchëv made no stipulation about conversion to communism so long as Moscow received political preference over America. His first serious opportunity arose in 1956 when
Anglo-French and Israeli forces botched their invasion of Egypt.

Fearing further Western attempts to depose him, President Gamal Abdel Nasser accepted the USSR's offer of financial credits as well as technical expertise. Millions of rubles and thousands of civil engineers were allocated for the construction of the Aswan dam. Military commanders were sent to retrain the Egyptian army and air force. Washington had opposed the Anglo-French-Israeli military adventure as soon as it heard of it, and President Eisenhower regretted the loss of Egypt to the growing "Soviet camp" of countries. For the same reason, Khrushchëv was cock-a-hoop about the acquisition of a client state of strategic importance.

The pattern was repeated elsewhere in the Middle East with the Soviet leadership presenting itself as the protector of national sovereignties against depredation by "international imperialism." Iraq, Syria, and Libya followed Egypt in accepting Moscow's aid programs. By the 1960s, the Middle East was a political tinderbox as the United States reinforced its alliances with Israel, Iran, and Saudi Arabia. Reluctant to go to war with each other, the two superpowers conducted a proxy military contest through their regional allies.

Neither America nor the Soviet Union was motivated by love for Islam and its believers. In particular, Moscow favored its "Muslim" client states precisely because they pursued secular, modernizing agendas at the expense of Islamic tradition—both Khrushchëv and Brezhnev believed that this was the most effective way to chart a route, however long and winding it might prove to be, to the goal of world communist revolution. Hafiz al-Assad in Syria, Saddam Hussein in Iraq, and Muammar Gaddafi in Libya pursued policies that the Kremlin judged to be "progressive." They built up institutions of universal education, ensuring that secular technical subjects like mathematics and engineering were to the fore. They gave opportunities for professional advancement to women as well as to men and removed the obligation to wear customary Muslim clothing. They encouraged a commitment to the state in preference to ties to family or mosque. They challenged the American predilection for Israel and Saudi Arabia in the Middle East's regional rivalries. For Soviet rulers this was more than enough to justify the outlay of expertise and money to prop up the regimes of their clients.

Moscow had to pay a political price. Nasser, Assad, Hussein, and Gaddafi ruthlessly suppressed their national communist parties, tolerating no rival political organization. The Kremlin, prioritizing the quest for allies who stood up to the United States, turned a blind eye to the arrest and torture of communist militants whom it had subsidized. Truly, it was a serpentine road to the goal of global communist utopia.

There were also costs that Moscow had not budgeted for. When a coalition of Arab states attacked Israel in 1967, the Israeli army was more than a match for them, wrenching large patches of territory from the control of Egypt, Syria, and Jordan. This had the effect of increasing Egyptian and Syrian dependence on Soviet economic and military assistance. Nasser's reputation never recovered from the debacle, and his successor, Anwar Sadat, Egyptian president from 1970, reasoned that an American alliance would offer Egypt better prospects than the arrangement with the USSR. Nevertheless, all was not lost for Soviet interests elsewhere in the Middle East, and ties with Syria, Iraq, and Libya were strengthened. The USSR, moreover, benefited from a wholly unexpected source in 1973 when Saudi Arabia led a cabal of the oil-producing countries in jacking up the price of petrochemical supplies to world markets. Although Moscow was not privy to the commercial decision, it benefited in a dual fashion. The oil price hike caused an economic recession amid the United States and its Western allies while filling Moscow's coffers with vastly expanded revenues from the oil and gas that were coming on stream in Siberia and the Volga region and adding to the vast reserves in Azerbaijan. The Politburo was suddenly in a position to increase its aid to its foreign friends.

Under the surface of those Muslim societies undergoing "modernization," however, there lurked a deep resentment of the assault on tradition. The Soviet Union's allies were not the only countries to have this experience. The Pahlavi dynasty in Iran aimed at transforming its society and economy while aligning itself with the United States, and Shah Mohammad Reza Pahlavi showed the same repressive zeal as Assad, Hussein, and Gaddafi. The shah exiled his Muslim adversaries, including Ayatollah Khomeini, who denounced him as an irreligious, unpatriotic American puppet. The Pahlavis, unlike the kings of Saudi Arabia, did not place Islam at the core of their governing ideology any more than Assad, Hussein, and Gaddafi did. All four rulers presided over economies that gave precedence to state ownership in the petrochemical sector. But whereas the others looked to Moscow for assistance, the shah relied on Washington— and Washington gave him steady, uncritical support.

The Kremlin saw no reason for concern about its Middle Eastern client states, which appeared invulnerable to subversion if only they maintained their police-state harshness and their "progressive" social policies. Moscow continued to supply them with their requirements in military technology and training and to propagate the case that the American alliances with Israel, Saudi Arabia, and Egypt posed a threat to peace across the Middle East. The rivalry between the USSR and the United States attracted greater attention around the world than religious trends that were developing among their respective client states, as Islam of a radically reactionary nature made inroads into popular opinion. In Iran, the radical critics were headed by followers of the Shia cleric Khomeini; in Iraq and Egypt it was underground Sunni groups that led them. Governing regimes were increasingly fearful of being swept aside by an Islamic fundamentalist movement. The first to experience this fate was Iran, where the shah was deposed in February 1979 and replaced by Khomeini, who returned from exile in Paris. At least one superpower, America, had to recognize that support for Muslim powers could backfire on the supporter.

The Politburo declined to learn its lesson even though it possessed a larger number of academic and political advisers on the Middle East than any other country. Prominent among them was Evgeni Primakov, who was fluent in Arabic. Primakov rose to be deputy director of the Institute of World Economy and International Relations and then director of the Oriental Studies Institute. The intelligence services, too, kept a sharp eye on the Middle East, making their analyses regularly available to the political leadership; and the numerous Soviet technical experts based in Iraq, Syria, and Libya had a valuable acquaintance with the world of Islam. The problem was that every official had to phrase reports in terms that accorded with official policy. Brezhnev and his leading comrades imposed a framework that made it well-nigh impossible to speak truth to power.

The makers of Moscow's foreign policy, buoyed up by the bonanza of oil and gas revenues, became globally more adventurous. The Soviet military-industrial complex achieved something close to technological parity in the air and under the oceans with America, and Brezhnev took pride in pulling off an agreement with President Richard Nixon for a détente in relations between the superpowers. And yet—while they concurred about the need to avoid the outbreak of a third world war—America and the USSR continued to compete for influence around the globe. Moscow subsidized "national-liberation movements" in Latin America and Africa on the same basis as it had already contracted to do in the Middle East. It subsidized communist parties wherever they existed, including in client states which were hunting down and executing communists. At a time when the United States remained trapped in economic difficulties after the Saudi-inspired oil price hike of 1975, Kremlin spokesmen delivered a mortal diagnosis for "world capitalism." Moscow's view was that the long-predicted death of the global market economy was imminent and that communism was on the brink of achieving its permanent triumph.

Even so, the burden of the arms race still bore down heavily on the USSR's budget. The Americans were undeniably superior in technological dynamism and in agricultural competence. Eastern Europe was collapsing into the grip of Western bankers. Despite the brio of their foreign policy making since the mid-1970s, the communist leaders were disturbed by thoughts about their many points of weakness in trying to compete on a level basis with the other superpower.

The Kremlin welcomed the Iranian revolution for its anti-American dimension. But the war that broke out in 1980 between Iran and Iraq posed a difficulty for the Soviet-Iraqi alliance. Moscow initially behaved with restraint. But by 1982, when the Iranians gained the upper hand and threatened to advance on Baghdad, the USSR felt the need to offer unequivocal support for Saddam Hussein's armed forces. It was a complex situation since the Americans had been angered by Khomeini's rhetoric as well as by the storming of their Tehran embassy and the seizure of their diplomats as hostages. The United States and other NATO powers readily supplied arms and encouragement to Saddam. This made for an exceptional instance in the Cold War when the world's two superpowers were helping the same military side. Saddam and Khomeini agreed to a ceasefire in 1988 only after accepting that their countries were utterly exhausted by the fighting and that neither of them could achieve victory. Moscow gained nothing from the war. It had earned Khomeini's burning hostility for supporting Saddam. It had also supplied advanced weaponry to Saddam on the basis of financial credits that were unlikely to be paid off in the foreseeable future. And Saddam, by taking weaponry from NATO powers, had demonstrated his unreliability as the USSR's client state.

There was also growing nervousness in Moscow about the possibility that America might cause trouble on the USSR's long southern border. Afghan communists had seized power in Kabul in 1978. Soviet intelligence sources suggested that Washington was aiming to subvert the new revolutionary administration with a view to breaking Afghanistan's ties to the USSR. The Afghan communist leaders pleaded for Moscow to rescue them. In December 1979, in the teeth of warnings given by the Soviet high command, the inner core of the Politburo prevailed upon the decrepit Brezhnev to send the Soviet Army from Termez in southern Uzbekistan into Afghan territory. Within a few months, the enormity of the task of military occupation became evident. Whereas the USSR's client states in the Middle East effected a symbiosis with Islam, the Afghan communist administration treated imams as the enemy while loudly proclaiming its own atheist doctrines. Resistance groups were quickly formed under religious auspices, and a jihad was proclaimed against apostate Afghans and their infidel foreign enforcers. As the war intensified, thousands of Soviet soldiers perished and billions of rubles were wasted.

Soviet politicians were learning the hard way about the resilience of Islam as a unifying force. Whereas the Afghan mujahidin were fighting for their faith and their country, Soviet troops were in Afghanistan only because the Kremlin had given the order. The Islamists were willing to struggle unto death even if daggers or ancient rifles were their only weapons. As it happened, their leaders increasingly had foreign assistance in the form of money, weaponry, and media support. The USSR had expected trouble from the Americans but was surprised by the impact of long-distance intervention by foreign Muslims. Wealthy Saudis and the Saudi government, as well as Pakistan's government and intelligence services, were determined to prevent the mujahidin from being crushed by Moscow's armed forces. The Soviet Army was capable of surviving the war but stood no chance of winning it.

Intimations of disaster piled pressure on the Politburo to reconsider the range of its policies. In 1980 Poland was boiling with anticommunist discontent. This involved a challenge to the Soviet domination of Eastern Europe if only because the USSR's ruined budget made it unrealistic for Moscow to occupy Warsaw as it had done in Kabul. The USSR's agricultural output was in irreversible decline. America's modernization of its strategic weapons system under Ronald Reagan, who entered the White House in 1981, compelled the Soviet leadership to allocate an additional budget to its military-industrial complex. Politburo members continued to hear reports that religious faith, including Islam, was gaining in appeal throughout the Soviet Union. Reform-minded leaders were beginning to wonder whether they could afford to disburse largesse to the world's communist and other left-wing parties and organizations. But although the diseases of current policy received a very roughly accurate diagnosis, nobody in the Kremlin as yet dared to propose a cure. Brezhnev died in 1982, and his successor, Yuri Andropov, died in 1984 before he could implement the slight renovation of external and internal policies that he thought necessary. His own successor, the singularly unimpressive Konstantin Chernenko, who had once been Brezhnev's chief of staff, put a stop to most of Andropov's timid initiatives. The Politburo was crossing its fingers and hoping for the best.

5

Perestroika and Its Complications

THINGS CHANGED ABRUPTLY WHEN MIKHAIL GORBACHËV became party general secretary in March 1985. He was putting himself forward as the doctor who would save the communist order in the USSR and resuscitate its power and prestige around the world. Over the next few years, he provided slogans for the treatment that he recommended: glasnost (open discussion), democratization, and perestroika (restructuring). The entire range of policy was transformed as Gorbachëv got to work.

He knew that he could make no progress without radical change in the ruling communist party. Officials appointed in the Brezhnev period were an unmistakable obstacle to reform, and a total revision of attitudes and practices was needed. Gorbachëv restored the requirement of elections to party office. This was the beginning of an earthquake in Soviet public affairs. As reform was piled upon reform, Gorbachëv announced that Moscow would no longer impose detailed supervision over local communist organizations or the agencies of local government. He equipped state enterprises with the freedom to operate outside the requirements of the State Planning Administration. He championed the right of all the USSR's nations to self-expression and autonomous development. When office holders in the party and government mounted passive resistance to his purposes, he turned for support to the creative intelligentsia. He altered the Soviet constitution to eliminate the party's dominant authority and to elevate himself to the presidency. His refrain was that total reform was overdue in the USSR. Gorbachëv claimed to be developing a new kind of socialism that would become the envy of the world.

His measures nonetheless had the effect of undermining the communist political and economic order. As administrative decentralization proceeded, the fifteen Soviet republics were left to their own devices so long as their leaders displayed at least the minimum of adherence to Gorbachëv's reform program. In the republics of the south Caucasus and central Asia, the communist leaders fawned on Gorbachëv as they once had displayed adulation to Brezhnev—and they consolidated their political grip by promoting the interests of their patronage networks. Gorbachëv was inadvertently reinforcing the disintegrative trends that had started under Brezhnev.

Furthermore, Gorbachëv's naïveté about the "national question" led to blunders in the matter of personnel appointments. One of his early mistakes occurred in December 1986 when he justifiably fired Kazakhstan's veteran communist leader Kunaev but replaced him with a Russian outsider, Gennadi Kolbin. Nobody could reasonably claim that Kunaev was mistreated, since his republic was a byword for corruption and he himself was a prime beneficiary. Nor were Russians an insignificant minority in Kazakhstan. Indeed, they constituted 38 percent of the population, whereas the Kazakhs were just short of 40 percent. But the Kazakh inhabitants had bitter memories of the 1930s when Stalin's policy of forcible "sedentarization" and agricultural collectivization had killed off half of the republic's population. They also resented how the demographic balance had been artificially shifted before and after World War II by the use of their country as a dumping ground for political prisoners as well as by the plowing up of its virgin lands by teams of Russian bulldozers and tractors. Kolbin's arrival affronted all Kazakh opinion, an opinion that had been silenced for many decades.

In December 1986, protests broke out in Kazakhstan's capital, Almaty. Hundreds of Russian residents suffered violent abuse before the armed forces restored order. Although Kolbin held on to his post until 1989, Kazakhs in the communist political establishment of the republic increasingly cooperated with Kazakh nationalists and Muslim clerics who castigated the Moscow leadership for its past treatment of the Kazakh people. This was not a phenomenon confined to Kazakhstan. Communist elites throughout central Asia and the Caucasus, while ostensibly remaining loyal to Gorbachëv's policies, saw advantage in identifying themselves with the particular nations which they ruled. The process of political nationalization made an ever deeper imprint.

Even so, Gorbachëv maintained his commitment to decentralization and democratization. It is true that in November 1986 he gave a speech in Tashkent telling the Uzbekistan communist leadership to "reinforce atheist propaganda among the masses" to counteract Islam, but this was one of his last flings as a communist doctrinaire. He soon came to change his general approach to religion. Gorbachëv thought it imperative to convince everyone that the authorities intended to rule in a more open-minded, flexible fashion than any of his predecessors. He enthused many fellow citizens, encouraging a rise of the communist party membership to a peak of twenty-one million. Although he continued to profess himself a Marxist, his course of policy also fostered conditions in which people of all beliefs could worship and proselytize freely. The Russian Orthodox Church received special indulgence, and Gorbachëv, despite his atheist convictions, took part in the millennial celebrations of the country's

Christianization in 1988. Quietly, the pressure was lessened on the other faiths and denominations, including Islam.

Applications were made to reopen long-closed mosques and prayer houses. Attendance rapidly increased, and clerics who had weathered the years of religious persecution gained public recognition. Sermons were delivered about communism's doom and the inevitable victory of Islam. The widening limits of glasnost allowed the publication of the Koran in the USSR's local languages—a process that was strengthened by the availability of Saudi Arabian subsidies. (In any previous Soviet decade, financial support from abroad would have been treated as illegal, and those in receipt of it would have been subject to arrest as counterrevolutionary subversives.) The Saudis had smaller success in spreading Wahhabi doctrines—their stern, intolerant interpretation of Islam—in Tatarstan and Dagestan than had been the case in Afghanistan. But it was a different matter in Tajikistan, where many Sunni Muslims responded with enthusiasm to Wahhabism. The Islamic renaissance was a diverse phenomenon across the USSR, but everywhere there was a freshness of thought and action among Muslim believers. Imams announced that Islam was experiencing a great awakening.

There were many instances in the Muslim-inhabited territories of central Asia and the Caucasus where anti-Russian feelings and Islamic fervor were entwined—and trouble was never far from the surface. In 1990 the Islamic Revival Party (IRP) was founded in Astrakhan at a time when several other political parties were emerging in the USSR. The IRP declared its aim to unite all Muslims regardless of nationality and to reform the economy not as Gorbachëv wanted but on the basis of sharia law.

Russian nationals were not the only victims of violence as Soviet Azerbaijan subsided into turmoil. Clashes erupted between Azeris and Armenians over the Armenian enclave of Nagorno-Karabakh; attacks on Armenian inhabitants of the Azerbaijani capital of Baku provoked Gorbachëv in January 1990 to send in troops to restore peace and stability. The Soviet Army killed scores of civilians. As had happened in Almaty in 1986, the Baku repression exacerbated national resentment. Communists, moreover, found themselves competing for influence against Islamic organizations that no longer operated in secret. Marxism-Leninism was routinely denounced by Muslim spokesmen. Although open calls for the breakup of the USSR remained few and far between, discontent with Moscow spread as Gorbachëv's incompetent economic reforms served to destroy the workings of the old retail trade without installing a viable alternative. Likewise, his democratizing measures wrecked the administrative order while omitting to introduce a reliable new one. Kazakhs, Azeris, Uzbeks, and Chechens—as well as many other Muslim peoples—railed against Soviet politicians who were lamentable in the provision of the basic material requisites of life.

In the midst of all this from the mid-1980s, Gorbachëv changed the basis of Soviet foreign and security policy by reaching out to President Ronald Reagan to join in a search for world peace. Reagan had long searched for ways to eliminate or at least reduce nuclear weapon stockpiles. From their first summit in Geneva in December 1985, Reagan and Gorbachëv agreed on the need for an enhanced process of negotiation. The two superpowers advanced to accords on armaments reduction, and the USSR began to make itself more acceptable to America in policies on human rights and the Third World. By 1989, when Gorbachëv met Reagan's successor, President George H. W. Bush, off the coast of Malta, both sides accepted that the Cold War was over.

One roadblock to reconciliation between America and the USSR had been the Soviet invasion of Afghanistan. Reagan made it clear that military withdrawal was a prerequisite for the Americans to come to terms on other important matters. It took time for him to recognize that Gorbachëv genuinely intended to pull his forces out of a war that Brezhnev's high command had never wanted and that was draining Gorbachëv's budget at a time when oil and gas prices were plunging on the world market. Coming to the Politburo, Gorbachëv read out doleful letters from soldiers' mothers, and there was unanimous agreement with him on the desirability of finding a way to leave Afghanistan without loss of face. The Afghan Islamic fighters, or mujahidin, intensified their jihad, aided by American supplies of Stinger handheld missiles that enabled them to down Soviet helicopters. Gorbachëv and his foreign affairs minister, Eduard Shevardnadze, vainly pleaded with the Americans not to strengthen the mujahidin. Reagan declined to ease Gorbachëv's plight: the old Politburo had made its bloody bed, and now the new one had to lie in it. After arduous talks in Vienna, a deal was made for an orderly withdrawal, and the Soviet Army marched back into the USSR in 1989. The Soviet leadership had discovered that foreign military occupation, far from weakening Islamic radicalism, strengthened it.

In the same year, Gorbachëv and Shevardnadze fundamentally revised official policy on client states in the rest of Asia. In the winter of 1988–89, Shevardnadze set off on a multicountry trip to spread the news that allies should no longer count upon Soviet assistance to defend them against their external enemies. He and Gorbachëv recognized that if Moscow wanted to have friendlier ties with Washington and Beijing, it had to end its active support for those countries that annoyed either of them. The Chinese objected to the Vietnamese, whom they accused of perpetual belligerence; the Americans spoke of Iraq, Libya, and Syria as threats to peace in the Middle East—and the Soviet leadership accepted that it no longer made sense to antagonize the Saudis and Israelis if it hoped to be welcomed as Washington's partner in cooling down the Asian hot spots. It was also crucial for Gorbachëv and Shevardnadze to block the drain on the USSR's budget that flowed from the help that it rendered to Middle Eastern client states—Iraq was only the worst of them in borrowing more than it ever paid back. The era of informal subsidy was to be brought to an end.

Hafiz al-Assad in Syria and Saddam Hussein in Iraq reacted to the news with incredulity, having always felt that they could depend on the USSR; Assad moaned to Shevardnadze that he had once been a grateful visiting student in Moscow. But there was nothing that they could do to change Gorbachëv's mind, and Shevardnadze sped off to Iran where he held talks with Ayatollah Khomeini. Hussein had bid him an ironic farewell: "May Allah help you. Only let it be our Allah and not the Iranian one!" The purpose of Shevardnadze's trip was to effect a rapprochement with Iran despite the militant Islamic revolution that the Shia clergy were conducting. Khomeini asserted Iran's pride and independence by refusing to talk to Shevardnadze in Tehran and insisting on meeting him in his modest, ill-kept house in Qom. The ayatollah adopted a gruff, uncompromising tone. Sensing that communism was on an irreversible decline, he sent Gorbachëv a letter calling on him to see the light and adopt Islam as the true faith. Assad and Hussein had shared this pessimism about Gorbachëv's political prospects even though they forbore to express this directly to him or Shevardnadze. Throughout the Middle East the feeling grew that the Soviet Union's days in the sun were coming to an end.

Gorbachëv laughed off Khomeini's advice and expressed confidence about the USSR's future if only he could impose his reformed variety of communism. He also assumed that he had an understanding with President George H. W. Bush about enabling the two superpowers to resolve international disputes on a peaceful basis. The disarmament treaties signed with Reagan and Bush appeared to certify the supremacy of diplomacy over the use of force. In Gorbachëv's eyes, this would be the foundation stone of a new world order.

Events in the Middle East soon pointed in a different direction. In August 1990, Iraq's Saddam Hussein invaded and annexed neighboring Kuwait. President Bush, with enthusiastic backing in Congress, issued a string of ultimatums warning that America would lead a military coalition to expel the Iraqi occupiers unless Saddam immediately withdrew his forces. Gorbachëv and Shevardnadze pushed at the United Nations for the prolongation of talks with Baghdad. When Gorbachëv discovered that Shevardnadze sympathized with the Americans, he dispatched Primakov—the academic Arabist turned public figure—to implore Saddam in person to appreciate the dangers of the situation. Gorbachëv sent his own letters pleading with the Iraqi dictator to comply with the UN Security Council's demand for immediate withdrawal from Kuwait. Meanwhile, the Soviet economic crisis sharpened. Shevardnadze had suggested exploring the possibility of raising billions of dollars in loans from the Saudis as a means of bailing out the sinking Soviet budget. Gorbachëv was caught between searching for external financial assistance and refusing to condone the use of force against Saddam.

The reality was that Bush already preferred military action to diplomacy. War commenced in January 1991 and was over in a few weeks after America and its allies carried out a bombing campaign that destroyed Iraq's forces. The result, however, was a gruesome mess in the Middle East that brought instant disappointment to the USSR and decades of frustration to the Americans. Although Kuwait was liberated, Saddam remained in power and could continue to cause trouble because Bush had decided not to destabilize Iraq further by occupying Baghdad. As for Gorbachëv, his objective of becoming friends with every state in Asia, including Israel and Saudi Arabia, had produced only marginal gains.

When Gorbachëv failed to obtain sufficient foreign loans to plug the gaping hole in his budget, the opposition to his leadership swelled in the USSR. Public criticism had been liberated by his democratizing policies. Party and government officials sensed the imminent collapse of the entire Soviet order. In the various republics, including Russia itself, the national communist elites became accustomed to handling affairs without recourse to Moscow. There was consternation in Moscow, where most members of the leading group around Gorbachëv concluded that his removal was necessary to preserve the USSR as a centralized state. In August 1991, they held him in detention in Crimea, pretended that he had fallen ill, and proclaimed a State Committee of the Emergency Situation. This was a coup in all but name, and most of the republican leaders quickly declared in its favor. Nearly all the "Muslim" republics obeyed the State Committee, with only President Nursultan Nazarbaev of Kazakhstan siding with Russia's President Boris Yeltsin in defying the plotters. Yeltsin's intervention turned the tide against the State Committee, and the coup leaders lost all their nerve and morale. On the third day, the State Committee was dissolved, its members being taken into custody.

Although Gorbachëv returned from Crimea to resume the USSR presidency, it was Russian president Yeltsin who set the agenda throughout the fall and early winter months of 1991. After Ukraine voted in a referendum for full independence, Yeltsin concluded that his best option was to dismantle the federal state structure of the USSR and implement complete Russian independence. To this end, in early December he helped arrange a meeting with Ukraine's President Leonid Kravchuk, Belorussia's Stanislaŭ Shushkevich, and Kazakhstan's Nursultan Nazarbaev at a state holiday dacha deep in Belorussia's Belovezha Forest. Nazarbaev flew from Almaty but stopped over in Moscow, where Gorbachëv persuaded him against joining the others, apparently by offering him the chairmanship of the USSR Supreme Soviet. Meanwhile, in the Belovezha Forest a drastic decision was made to break up the USSR and replace it with a Commonwealth of Independent States. Nazarbaev's absence meant that none of the politicians who designed the project hailed from a "Muslim" and non-Slavic Soviet republic. When the news was communicated to Gorbachëv, he made one last effort to thwart Yeltsin. But as he quickly discovered, he had lost the last props of adequate support. On December 25, 1991, he went on TV to announce his resignation and the dismantlement of the USSR.

6

The Islamic Question in the Russian Federation

A S   T H E   F I F T E E N   S O V I E T   R E P U B L I C S   W E R E   R E A L I Z I N G their independence, Yeltsin set about exercising political control and fostering economic recovery in the Russian Federation. His government's measures included price liberalization as a first step toward the introduction of a free market in goods and services. Yeltsin pronounced an anathema on communism, describing the Soviet decades as a totalitarian nightmare. Western leaders welcomed him as once they had done with Gorbachëv.

Trouble quickly arose for Yeltsin as his supporters split into factions. The old Russian Soviet Constitution remained in force and gave political weight to the Russian Supreme Soviet, where a majority of deputies sought to slow the transition to a market economy and to restrict Yeltsin's authority as president. Matters came to a head in the fall of 1993, when Yeltsin reacted to an armed outburst of opposition in Moscow by surrounding the "Russian White House"—seat of the Supreme Soviet—and arresting his vice president, Alexander Rutskoi, and the other ringleaders. In the continuing economic and political turmoil, Yeltsin's popularity dipped and Russia entered years of industrial contraction and financial recession. Only the even greater difficulties faced by the other countries of the Commonwealth of Independent States made Russian conditions seem at all survivable. The standard of living for most Russians plummeted. Yeltsin had to appeal to a group of ultra-rich businessmen for the campaign funds and media support he needed to win the 1996 presidential election. In return he promised to deliver some of Russia's oil reserves and other natural resources into their control. The deal was sealed, and Yeltsin, despite being physically ailing, gained electoral victory over the resurgent Russian communists.

Throughout these years, Yeltsin assured Muslim citizens of the Russian Federation that they would always enjoy complete civic equality under the rule of law. This principle was embedded in the new constitution, which was confirmed by referendum in December 1993. Freedom of religious expression and observance was integral to the administration's stated purposes and—for a while—to its actions. Imams were often viewed on national TV channels giving morning homilies—there was nothing like this in any other European or North American country. It was by such means that the vast majority of Russians who were not of the Muslim faith received their first direct acquaintance with the nature of Islam. The televised imams were calm, measured, and presentable. Among them was Talgat Tadzhuddin, a Kazan-born Tatar who had trained in Bukhara and Cairo and gained recognition as the chief mufti of Russia and leader of the Central Muslim Spiritual Directorate. He professed loyalty to the Russian legal order and preached against the political exploitation of Islam. In return, he obtained endorsement for his religious activities. Drawing attention to people like Tadzhuddin, Yeltsin declared Russia to be a truly pluralist society.

He had a point. By the time of the 2002 census, there were said to be twenty million Muslims in the Russian Federation. This would have meant that out of 144 million citizens, roughly 15 percent were Islamic believers, mostly but not exclusively of non-Russian ethnic ancestry. As is usual with such calculations, there may have been some overestimation because some of the "Muslims" did not identify themselves as such and had been assigned to the Islamic faith because of their ethnicity. It made no more sense to call every Kabardinian a Muslim—especially if the individual in question had never said an Islamic prayer or visited a mosque—than it did to designate all Russians as Christians. This question of numbers has become controversial. According to one reasonable estimate, those who voluntarily call themselves Muslim might amount to between three million and nine million people. It is disconcerting that so wide a gap exists between the lower and higher number. Furthermore, the same estimate does not include the many migrant workers from neighboring Muslim-inhabited countries, who may total 1.5 million. But though the Islamic demographic presence remains a matter of some dispute, it is beyond dispute that Muslims are a very substantial and growing minority.

By far, the greatest proportion of them belongs to the Sunni branch of Islam; only 5 percent are Shia. Nevertheless, as happens elsewhere, there is much diversity inside and outside both of the main branches of the faith. In Dagestan and Chechnya, the gentle traditions of Sunni Sufism survive, including devotion to shrines of saints—traditions that Salafi clerics, influenced by Saudi religious intolerance, condemn as idolatry. Moreover, Russia has many Ahmadi Muslims. Diversification is on the increase because as Azeris migrated from Azerbaijan to make their living in Russia, they brought their Shia doctrines with them.

Conditions for Russian Muslims, regardless of their branch of Islam, changed drastically after the fall of communism. They could travel abroad so long as they could assemble the money. Whereas other citizens went on holiday to Cyprus and other sunny climes, Muslim believers joined the annual hajj to Mecca. This pilgrimage is an obligation for the world's Muslims at least once in their lifetimes, but it was only in the 1990s that it became a widespread requirement for Russia's Muslims. Mosques and madrasas were constructed throughout the country. The Koran went on sale in street stalls. Muslims tried to live their lives by Islamic precepts. It was inevitably a patchy process, and Ravil Gainutdin, head of the Council of Muftis, lamented the low level of spiritual awareness among the Muslims of Tatarstan: "The Tatars marry Russians and then have their children christened. At the [ancient Tatar] Sabantui festival they indulge in vodka and pork dishes. Eighty per cent of those who attend the mosques are refugees who don't know the Tatar language and ask for preaching to be read out in Russian." In several parts of the north Caucasus there has been only fitful Islamic education over many decades, and the older mullahs were often worsted in dispute by younger, radical preachers.

As he had promised before taking power, Yeltsin permitted the Russian Federation's regions to deepen the process of de-communization without interference. His policy was warmly received in Tatarstan and Bashkortostan, which were Muslim-inhabited zones with valuable natural resources in oil and gas. The republican leaders Mintimer Shaimiev and Murtaza Rakhimov courted their Muslim voters by subsidizing the construction of religious edifices and supporting Islamic charities. Kazan and Ufa, the capitals of Tatarstan and Bashkortostan, surpassed the level of importance they had had as Muslim regional centers under the tsars. Shaimiev in particular displayed a notable self-confidence, dominating the Tatarstani elites and founding a political cult for himself as he headed the appeal to refurbish the Qolşärif Mosque in the Kazan Kremlin. (The building was opened to huge fanfare in 2005.) Tatarstan adopted Islamic symbolism in its public monuments and architecture. Publications in the Tatar language flourished as never before, many of the newspapers and books had an Islamic content, and the Kazan TV stations broadcast programs on Islam.

Tatars, according to the 2002 census, made up 52 percent of Tatarstan's population. Though Shaimiev relied upon their electoral support, he also looked after the rest of the population, including Russians who constituted two-fifths of the republic's population. Such was his popularity that in 1992 he felt able to reject the draft Federal Treaty because he wanted a looser linkage to Moscow than Yeltsin proposed. Two years of wrangling followed before a mutually acceptable constitutional compromise was attained. Shaimiev made himself useful to Yeltsin by making life difficult for the nascent Ittifaq party, which called for the establishment of an Islamic state in the Volga region. Yeltsin and Shaimiev at least shared a determination to stamp out the flames of religious fundamentalism before they could become a blaze.

Yeltsin had met with greater trouble in Chechnya since November 1991, when Major-General Dzhokar Dudaev was elected as the republic's president. He declared its breakaway from Russia while the USSR still existed and Russia was still a Soviet republic—and Gorbachëv turned down Yeltsin's request for troops to be deployed against the secessionists. Dudaev, like Shaimiev in Tatarstan, had once been a communist party member; he had also been on military service in Afghanistan, winning the Order of the Red Star for valor against the mujahidin. But he had spent his childhood with Chechen deportees in Kazakhstan. As commander of a strategic bomber base in Soviet Estonia, he had won praise from the Estonians for ignoring orders to close down the Tallinn TV station. On becoming Chechen president, Dudaev presented himself as a fervent Muslim and ignored those who reminded him of his bombing exploits against Islamic fighters in the Afghan war. Chechens warmed to a compatriot who annoyed Moscow. Dudaev built mosques as eagerly as Shaimiev and Rakhimov. Yeltsin saw that whereas the rulers of Tatarstan and Bashkortostan played the old double game of praising the Kremlin while quietly pursuing their own ambitions, Dudaev appeared at his happiest when teasing the Russian government.

Dudaev claimed more for Chechnya than Shaimiev dared in Tatarstan or Rakhimov in Bashkortostan: absolute independence. He also engineered a split from neighboring Ingushetia; until 1992, the two republics were equal parts of a unified Chechno-Ingushetia. The scale of growing official corruption and organized crime was remarkable, and political opposition intensified. Dudaev was inept at imposing order despite his martial background, but he somewhat widened his support by allowing the spread of sharia law.

In December 1994 Yeltsin in exasperation ordered the aerial bombardment of Grozny and sent in ground troops to establish control. Dudaev fled his presidential residence and regrouped his loyal forces in the south of the republic. He bragged that Chechens would fight a guerrilla war from their mountains even if defeated in conventional warfare. Russian Deputy Defense Minister Boris Gromov, who in 1989 had been the last Soviet soldier to leave Afghanistan across the Friendship Bridge into Tajikistan, forecast that the bloody Afghan quagmire was about to be repeated, and he resigned in protest. Throughout 1995, Dudaev's bands picked off Russian Army units. In April 1996, however, Dudaev was killed by a laser-guided missile after a Russian reconnaissance plane detected him using his satellite phone. In August, as the number of casualties rose on both sides, Chechens and Russians agreed to a truce. Yeltsin recognized that he had made a grievous mistake in starting the war, and an uneasy peace held. But Chechens had not given up their desire for independence, and the Russian administration contained many who resented the fact that Chechnya had avoided complete reconquest.

Dudaev had designated Islam as the state religion, and his successors Zelimkhan Yandarbiev and Aslan Maskhadov went further in indulging the Islamic radicals. Soon it was evident that imported Wahhabi or Salafi doctrines were overtaking Sufism in political and financial influence. Militants campaigned against the age-old practices of worship at Sufi holy shrines. Maskhadov came to see that this offended many Chechens, but he was unable to prevent the rise of religious fundamentalism. As radicals under Shamil Basaev conducted terrorist bombings and abductions elsewhere in the Russian Federation, including Dagestan, the armed movement for independence was resumed in Chechnya. The Chechen question became associated in Russia's public opinion with extremist Islamist violence, while Russian military countermeasures provoked revulsion among foreign Muslims. An already bad situation became drastically worse.

Yeltsin did little to stem the drift toward local measures of discrimination against Muslims. The Moscow city administration issued a decree that restricted the influx of migrants in quest of economic self-betterment. The principal targets were individuals from the north and south Caucasus as well as from central Asia. Ethnic Russian residents complained about the skyrocketing cost of goods in the new market economy, and there were claims that a disproportionate number of the new small traders were not Russians but "Caucasians" who were charging exorbitant prices. There was also widespread resentment about the tide of immigrants seeking jobs as manual workers and pressing down average wage levels. For a few weeks, it became hazardous for persons who looked as if they were from the Caucasus to walk the streets. As violent attacks by Russian thugs proliferated, there were occasional arrests. But the police were widely less than efficient in imposing the rule of law, especially in an environment where pride in Russian nationhood was becoming a feature of governmental propaganda.

Even so, it was still a complex situation, and Muslim political and religious leaders remained assertive. When in 1998 the idea was mooted of publishing a Russian translation of Salman Rushdie's novel *The Satanic Verses*, several of Russia's Muslim leaders declared that the publishers and the translator would be putting their physical safety in jeopardy. Their feeling was that Muslims had the right to take action against being offended despite the constitutional guarantees of freedom of expression. In the same year, when tensions rose between Muslim and Christian believers, the Russian Orthodox Church initiated a regular forum, the Inter-Religious Council of Russia, to stop the growing trend toward conflict.

War came again to Chechnya in 1999 when Vladimir Putin, the last in Yeltsin's line of prime ministers, hardened the case for military action by accusing Chechen Islamist radicals of carrying out terrorist attacks in central Russia. Explosions took place in Dagestan and Moscow, and Putin claimed that a further attempt had been foiled in an apartment block in Ryazan. The Russian Army was ordered into Chechnya, and its capital, Grozny, was hammered by air strikes. Chechen leaders called themselves mujahidin and proclaimed a jihad. But they were outgunned by the Russians, and the military result was never in doubt. This time the Russian administration recognized the desirability of recruiting Chechen collaborators to govern obediently in its name. One such was Akhmad Kadyrov, who had been Chechnya's chief mufti in the 1990s and became acting head of the government in mid-2000. Kadyrov family members were widely known as committed separatists, and Kadyrov himself, educated in Islamic schools in Bukhara and Tashkent, had been an anti-Russian militia commander until he switched sides. Kadyrov had no reluctance about treating his Chechen enemies as harshly as the Russian generals had done in the nineteenth century. At the same time, he took pride as a Muslim cleric in funding the construction of mosques and other religious facilities.

7

Dealing with the "Near Abroad"

Yeltsin unexpectedly stood down from office at the end of 1999 and made Putin the acting president until such time as an election could be held. Putin easily secured victory at the polls and made clear his intention to provide firm leadership to restore order in Russia and regain the country's status as a great power. He quietly let it be known that he blamed Yeltsin for the disorderliness that persisted in the economy and public affairs.

On relations with the other ex-Soviet republics, however, there was continuity in policy. The Belovezha Forest accords signed by Yeltsin, Kravchuk, and Shushkevich on December 8, 1991, involved an agreement to create a Commonwealth of Independent States involving as many ex-Soviet republics as desired to belong. Armenia, Azerbaijan, Kazakhstan, Kyrgyzstan, Moldova, Turkmenistan, Tajikistan, and Uzbekistan committed themselves at an Almaty meeting thirteen days afterward. (Kazakhstan's Nazarbaev had by then become an enthusiast for the USSR's abolition.) Notable by their rejection of the opportunity to join the new commonwealth were the Baltic states of Estonia, Latvia, and Lithuania, as well as Georgia in the south Caucasus. Yeltsin had personally recognized the right of Soviet republics to their independence even before the USSR ceased to exist. He worked from the assumption that the Russian Federation would in some way or another succeed in dominating the territories that had been under Russian control for centuries. He was also determined that, sooner or later, Russia would achieve a political and economic recovery that would reestablish the country's status as a great power.

Yeltsin looked with concern at the "near abroad"—the term for other countries of the former Soviet Union. When Gorbachëv and Shevardnadze were arranging for the Soviet Army's withdrawal from Afghanistan, they warned the Americans about the danger of giving support to mujahidin; they had learned that jihad could acquire a life of its own and run out of control. The Islamist irregulars, despite being worse armed than Moscow's forces, had seen off the Soviet occupation—and religious fanaticism had provided a sharp edge. Afghan communist leader Mohammad Najibullah tumbled from power in 1992. After a bitter civil war, the fanatical Islamist Taliban under Mullah Muhammed Omar swept into power in Kabul four years later. This was not an outcome that Yeltsin could regard with equanimity as fears grew that jihadism might seep across the Afghan border into Tajikistan and beyond. Yeltsin provided support to the Afghan military leader Ahmad Shah Massoud in the civil war that was tearing Afghanistan apart. Massoud headed a force of mujahidin who had fought against the Soviet occupation, but his brand of Islamic fundamentalism was markedly more moderate than that of the Taliban under Mullah Omar. The Taliban reacted by declaring a jihad against Russia. Omar's statements were alarming even though he lacked the resources to put his threats into action.

The Commonwealth of Independent States was a formal arrangement, having no linkages that interfered with each member country's capacity to do as it liked within its borders. Yeltsin was not going to let any neighboring country damage Russia's interests, and Russian economic and military superiority allowed it to throw its weight about. He pragmatically supported the authoritarian rulers in central Asia and the Caucasus who were willing to cooperate with him. In most of these territories there was a seamless transition from communism to nationalism led by presidents who had been prominent communists. This was an early example of the limited nature of Yeltsin's commitment to democracy. For him, the important objective was to have leaders in the "near abroad" on whom he could rely, and he overlooked their authoritarianism and abuses of human rights.

The pattern in all these countries, with the exception of Christian Georgia and Armenia, was for ruling elites to embrace Islam and nationalism as they explored how to manage their independence. The governments in Uzbekistan and Tajikistan introduced a version of Arabic script instead of the Cyrillic one in official publications, but this quickly proved to be a step too far for administrators who had been brought up writing only Russian. All the rulers in former Soviet central Asia, moreover, remained alert to the danger of a spread of Islamic fundamentalism. While showering peaceful imams with respect and subsidies, the presidents of Kazakhstan, Tajikistan, Uzbekistan, Kyrgyzstan, and Turkmenistan policed their countries strictly and rooted out the fresh growth of religious extremism. The idea was not merely to outflank the jihadis but to eradicate them; Uzbekistan's President Islam Karimov was so anxious about the threat from Wahhabi ideas that in 1998 he banned women from wearing the hijab and men from sporting beards. Prevention, he argued, was better than cure. In Kyrgyzstan, President Askar Akaev established rules for the compulsory registration of mosques; fellow rulers elsewhere in the region universally did the same.

Kazakhstan's Nazarbaev, who from 1989 to 1991 had served as his republic's communist party leader, set about shaping policies that would fit Kazakhstan for its future after communism. He published a book, *Without Right and Left*, in which he promised to pursue the national interest regardless of ideology. Vast resources in oil were offered as an inducement to global petrochemical corporations to modernize the national facilities for extraction, refining, and transportation. Under pressure from Moscow, Nazarbaev allowed Russia's newly privatized companies to play a part, but he disappointed them in their ambition to dominate the market. He elevated the role of ethnic Kazakhs in the administration and the economy. Clan networks that had been strengthened in the Brezhnev and Gorbachëv years obtained ever fuller license. The Kazakh ruling group accrued immense wealth by corrupt manipulation of the political process, and Nazarbaev's close relatives became among the richest people in all Kazakhstan. The state ideology glorified the leader, lamenting the wrongs done to the Kazakh people under communist rule and lauding the benefits of a tolerant kind of Islam.

The large Russian minority had earlier been valued for its education and technical skills. Now Russians observed that when it came to a choice of a Kazakh or a Russian for promotion, the Kazakh was usually the winner. The result was a growing exodus of Russian families from Kazakhstan. As the country became re-Kazakhized, it was also re-Islamized. In politics, central authority was imposed and dissent was pulverized by the security agencies. Kazakhstan's jails operated with a total neglect of the welfare of detainees. Pro-democracy critics suffered, as did Islamist fundamentalists. Yeltsin and his ministers overlooked the abuses, concentrating instead on maximizing Russia's influence over Kazakhstan.

Azerbaijan was another country that simultaneously worried and reassured Russian ministers. Like the Kazakhs, Azeris speak a language intelligible to Turkey's citizens. Turkic languages were also spoken in Kazakhstan, Kyrgyzstan, Turkmenistan, Uzbekistan, and elsewhere in Russia and central Asia. Although there were differences in phonology, morphology, and syntax, the peoples of the new states could communicate without much difficulty. Turkey's influence was on the rise as its entrepreneurs seized fresh opportunities to do business. Turkish TV shows enjoyed popularity. While economic regeneration was very patchy in the former USSR, Turkey's trading prowess enabled entrée to country after country. Soon, the anxiety among Russian politicians and businessmen was that a Turkic commercial, cultural, and religious affiliation could tug the region away from Russia's orbit and pose an important challenge in the years ahead just as the Ottoman Empire had done for centuries and Enver Pasha and Sultan Said-Galiev had striven to do after the First World War. Old geopolitical calculations were being made in both Ankara and Moscow, as Azerbaijan's president Heydar Aliev was all too aware. Like Nazarbaev, he worked to exploit the situation.

Aliev had belonged to the All-Union Politburo until 1987 when Gorbachëv shunted him into retirement. After the USSR's disintegration, he boisterously reascended the ladder of power in Baku, where he had once been the republican communist party first secretary. In 1993, when divisions between Azerbaijan's main areas brought the country to the verge of civil war, he was hurriedly elected president because he seemed the one man capable of imposing peace and order. Aliev used oil revenues to enrich himself and his friends. He also subsidized mosques, madrasas, and imams. Islam flourished as had never been possible under tsar or commissar. Whereas Kazakh Muslims were predominantly Sunnis, most Azeris belonged to the Shia branch of the faith because Azerbaijan had belonged to Persia until the Russian conquest. The Azeris still upheld their Shia traditions. Tehran's overtures to Baku for a political and religious linkage served to feed Turkish fears about Iranian expansionism. The wily Aliev knew how to play Tehran and Ankara off each other as well as how to negotiate with the Russians, who wanted to gain a stake in the Caspian Sea oil reserves and to prevent the spread of Islamic radicalism. Unlike Iran or Saudi Arabia, Azerbaijan established diplomatic relations with Israel. Profit, nationhood, and security mattered to Baku, rather than religious intolerance.

Aliev had never boasted of a liberal reputation, whereas President Karimov of Uzbekistan had been a communist reformer and one of Gorbachëv's allies. This did not stop him from acting brutally against opponents such as the underground international Hizb ut-Tahrir organization, which heralded the imminence of a global caliphate. The sadism of Uzbek security services was notorious even by the standards of ex-Soviet central Asia. Yeltsin as usual took no notice as long as his neighbors suppressed jihadis and avoided damage to Moscow's interests.

The former Soviet republic that most agitated the Kremlin was Uzbekistan's eastern neighbor Tajikistan, where civil war broke out in 1992. Throughout the country, an itch was felt to settle old scores even before the bloodshed spilled over from the Afghan charnel house. Clan clashed with clan, and there were several regional disputes about ownership of the country's natural resources. Russian politicians worried about the possible growth and spread of jihadism even though Islamist organizations were weak at the time. Moscow propped up the side led by Rahmon Nabiev, who accommodated Russia's military and economic interests and opposed Islamic fundamentalists. The ex-Soviet garrison troops, instead of being withdrawn to Russia, were ordered to lend support to Nabiev. The defeated rebels crossed into northern Afghanistan in search of sympathy and weaponry. A truce was signed after months of further fighting. The new Tajik Supreme Council came under the leadership of Emomali Rahmonov, who secured the dispatch of a Russia-led peacekeeping force that mopped up the large patches of continuing armed resistance. Troops from Uzbekistan and Kazakhstan were also involved. Governments in ex-Soviet central Asia shuddered at the idea, however remote, of violent Islamists coming to power in the Tajikistani capital, Dushanbe.

But Tajik rebels who had fled across the Afghan border regrouped in refugee camps with a view to resuming the armed struggle. Clashes recurred in 1993 in which Russian soldiers were killed. This served to reinforce Russia's military commitment to Rahmonov's cause. The 201st Motorized Infantry Division had remained in Tajikistan after the Soviet Union's collapse, but Yeltsin accepted that more troops were needed. With his support, Rahmonov effectively became president in 1996.

The civil war had tribal and regional dimensions. Islamist violence also played a part after armed groups in Badakhshan announced their ambition to install a Wahhabi dictatorship throughout the state. The butchery was relentless. It is estimated that between 50,000 and 100,000 people perished and up to 1.2 million became internal refugees in Tajikistan as the governmental forces engaged in bouts of ethnic cleansing. Rahmonov survived in power, but only because he could turn to the Russian military contingent for the defense of the capital, Dushanbe, against the jihadis, who were reinforced by volunteers from over the border in northern Afghanistan. Yeltsin had judged that whatever happened in Tajikistan could have vital importance for Russia's interests. The civil war, in his eyes, had demonstrated that the central Asian borders were easy to breach and that the Afghan imbroglio could spread northward unless vigorous countermeasures were taken. The United Nations became involved, and in 1997 Yeltsin hosted a meeting in the Kremlin attended by Tajikistan's president Rahmonov, who signed an agreement to bring the civil war to an end. At this point, Rahmonov judged it wise to compromise and even gave seats in the government to the Islamic Revival Party of Tajikistan as a way of taming its radicalism.

In Moscow there was concern that the situation in Tajikistan and in other former Soviet republics of the region might be vulnerable to meddling from the Middle East. Each of these republics, like Russia itself, had rulers who treated high office as a market stall for personal enrichment. There was widespread popular resentment of corruption, maladministration, authoritarianism, injustice, and poverty— and the surviving secret Islamist groups knew how to exploit such feelings. Russian ministries and security agencies kept a watch for any sign that foreign Muslim powers might try to enlist friends from among the jihadists.

The reality was that Shia Iran was always unlikely to make headway with Tajiks, who spoke a language like Persian but were Sunnis rather than Shias. Consequently, Tehran had no interest in aiding the rebel side in the civil war. The Iranian leadership was anyway wary of offending Russian ministers at a time of its own diplomatic isolation and economic subjection to American sanctions. Tehran therefore used its influence to help with the peacemaking process and then confined itself to subsidizing the construction of religious premises and distributing the Koran. The Iranians were not the only ones who supported mosque-building in the ex-USSR. Saudi Arabia, too, poured funds into Tajikistan and other former Soviet republics with large Muslim populations just as it had done in Afghanistan during the Soviet military occupation. Grants were made available for bright young Muslims to receive training in Saudi Arabia. The Saudis followed their usual procedure of handing out money only to those willing to accept the Wahhabi variant of Islam, and they did little to prevent some of their citizens from joining the anti-Russian forces in Chechnya. Fundamentalist teaching was on the rise even where active jihadi organizations were few.

Moscow academic institutes of oriental studies and of ethnography warned that this was a situation that could run out of control. Primakov, who emerged from Gorbachëv's tutelage to become director of Russia's Foreign Intelligence Service through 1996 and then became minister of foreign affairs and prime minister, spoke of the desirability of preventive measures.

Yet Primakov and other Russian leaders, after the bitter Soviet experience in Afghanistan, trod carefully in their handling of the "near abroad" and the wider world. These were years when Russia's state budget was too weak to underpin an assertive foreign policy except in a few hot spots such as Tajikistan—and even there the scale of the military commitment was limited. The Russian Army fell into a weakened condition after the end of the Cold War. Officers and troops complained of poor housing and equipment. Even the nuclear forces were left without essential funding. Diplomats streamed out of the Ministry of Foreign Affairs, where their salaries were pitifully low in comparison with the potential rewards in the emergent market economy. Yeltsin had to ask the International Monetary Fund for loans and entreat Washington to look kindly on his government. Russia's economic woes continued as the policies of price liberalization and enterprise denationalization failed to reverse the falloff in gross national product. The low prices for oil and gas on world markets—at a time when the government was vitally dependent on revenues from these exports—further narrowed the options available to Yeltsin in Russian foreign policy.

Russia did not always cooperate with America. In the Middle East, Yeltsin pressed for a peaceful resolution of the problems left behind by the 1991 Gulf War. Primakov argued for Russia to return to a Soviet-style orientation toward seeking friends in Iraq. Yeltsin put some political distance between himself and President Bill Clinton by refusing to endorse some of America's demands on the Saddam regime at the UN Security Council. Saddam predictably wanted something more substantial from Moscow than honeyed words. But Yeltsin was issuing a signal to "the Muslim world" that one of the superpowers, albeit the weaker one, favored a gentler Middle Eastern policy than the Americans practiced.

The other instance was in the former Yugoslavia, where Yeltsin raised objections about the NATO forces that Clinton assembled to intervene in Bosnia in 1993–95 and in Kosovo in 1999 as inter-ethnic violence acquired an intensity unprecedented since the Second World War. The Russian government protested that insufficient effort had been invested in diplomacy and that military intervention was undesirable. Yeltsin sent Viktor Chernomyrdin to Berlin as his personal envoy to plead with Serbia's President Slobodan Milosević to come to terms with the Americans and avert the bombing of his capital, but to no avail. America, the world's hyper-power, led a coalition that had vastly superior armaments, and its repeated raids forced Milosević from power. The most that Russia could do was to snipe from the sidelines. Incidentally, its forlorn attempt to moderate the assault on Milosević and the Serbian governing elite involved a downplaying of Serbia's maltreatment of the Muslims of Bosnia and Kosovo. The Serbian nation was mainly of the Orthodox Christian faith, and Yeltsin looked well on them just as Nicholas II had done before the First World War. Muslims in the Yugoslav lands had no reason to thank him.

Russian policies in Europe and Asia were conditioned by Yeltsin's calculations about the national interest, not by moral criteria or a desire to alleviate the plight of religious communities. Realpolitik ruled.

8

The Recovery of Russian External Confidence

Y ELTSIN'S GROWING ASSERTIVENESS IN WORLD POLItics paled in comparison with how his successor Vladimir Putin behaved. Even so, it took time for Putin to gauge the available opportunities. He began by searching for a beneficial friendship with the America of President George W. Bush while stressing that Russia was a "European" power eager to share European values and find ways to cooperate with European states. Of foreign leaders, Bush and Britain's Prime Minister Tony Blair were his most frequent confidants.

Putin's stance was put to the test after September 11, 2001, when a terrorist gang that consisted largely of Saudi citizens hijacked planes and destroyed the twin towers of the World Trade Center in New York. The inspiration and planning had come from the al-Qaida organization led by Osama bin Laden in the mountains of Afghanistan. Bin Laden subsidized the Taliban government of Mullah Omar in Kabul; Omar reciprocated by permitting al-Qaida to maintain a religious and terrorist training base in the country. When Omar refused to break with bin Laden, Bush decided to eradicate the threat by invasion. The NATO military coalition undertook an air and ground operation that overwhelmed the Taliban government, driving both Omar and bin Laden into hiding. The fighting was quickly over, and the Americans and their allies blithely assumed that all that was required was to eradicate the scattered jihadis and quickly organize democratic elections. To Russians, the American attitude appeared—and was—completely unrealistic. Russian think tanks had learned from the Soviet Army's experiences in 1979–89 that the military occupation of a Muslim country, especially one with an abundance of jihadis, was likely to prove disastrous for the occupiers.

Nevertheless, Putin shared the zeal to exterminate jihadi terrorism wherever it arose and raised no objection to the US Air Force using landing and refueling facilities in Uzbekistan. He thought of this as an act of extraordinary generosity in Russia's backyard. About one point, though, he was adamant: he was not going to let Russian armed forces become embroiled in the campaign. He probably also thought that if the Americans wished to get dragged into the Afghan morass, Russians could sit back and quietly laugh at their naïveté. If this was his attitude, it did not last very long. Steadily his irritation grew about Western criticism of the atrocities carried out by his forces in the war in Chechnya. Even his friends George W. Bush and Tony Blair lectured him. He regarded this as deeply ungrateful in the light of his helpfulness about Afghanistan. His was a simple viewpoint: having delivered help to the Western powers when they wanted it, he expected to have a free hand in dealing with Russia's Islamist terrorists and emphasized that Chechnya was the business of Russia and Russia alone.

Putin queried the sense in continuing to accommodate himself to Washington's policies. Russia's budget no longer depended on the IMF after the upsurge of world market oil and gas prices from

1999. Like Brezhnev in the mid-1970s, Putin benefited from the latest vagaries in global trade and could set about balancing the Russian budget. He gained the revenues to build up his military capacity, to boost the state welfare program, and to secure his political position at home and abroad.

Denouncing what he saw as American pretensions to world hegemony, Putin espoused the objective of establishing a global environment of "multipolar" politics. He laid emphasis upon each country's right to sovereignty. His ultimate wish was to ensure that nobody could interfere in Russian politics, and it was in this spirit that he reached out to those foreign states that were under pressure from America and its allies. In 2002 he criticized the UN-sponsored economic sanctions against Iraq. Putin, posing as a humanitarian who was interested only in saving Iraqi lives, offered to mediate in the diplomatic conflict between Washington and Baghdad. With equal persistence he opposed American plans for military action to compel the removal of weapons of mass destruction. President Bush nevertheless secured a UN Security Council resolution threatening "serious consequences" if Saddam refused to comply. Congress thereupon authorized an invasion. Frantic negotiations took place in the Security Council, with Britain aligning itself with America while France rejected the American case for war. Putin repeatedly argued that only peace talks under the United Nations' auspices ought to be used to settle the Iraq question.

In March 2003 an American-led military coalition crossed into Iraqi territory. Within three weeks it had taken Baghdad and driven Saddam into hiding until he was apprehended at the end of the year. While Bush celebrated the destruction of a brutal, expansionist dictatorship, Putin castigated the war as an affront to UN Security Council policy as well as to international opinion, and he reminded everyone that no weapons of mass destruction remained in Iraq at the time of the invasion. He turned down the invitation to meet Paul Bremer, the head of the Coalition Provisional Administration.

Even so, Putin had not succeeded in preventing America from going to war and was determined to avert a repetition in international conflicts. As a way of demonstrating Russia's capacity to act independently on the world stage, he turned toward Primakov's orientation in Middle Eastern policy. One of his first steps was to give a flattering speech to the Organization of the Islamic Conference in October 2003. Two years later, with Saudi Arabia's support, Russia gained observer status at the conference. In 2005, on a brief stopover in Chechnya, he proclaimed Russia as the defender of Islam worldwide. Foreign Affairs Minister Sergei Lavrov declared that "deeper relations of friendship and cooperation with the Islamic world are [now] Russia's strategic course. That is why we note with pleasure that . . . our constructive cooperation with the Muslim world [has] acquired a new dynamic." His prose was even more leaden than usual, as if he felt nervous about saying anything so transparently manipulative. Russian foreign policy on Islam was directed at exploiting the opportunities available since early 1991 when an America-led military coalition attacked a Muslim state in the Middle East.

As Baghdad and other Iraqi cities descended into turmoil, Syria and Iran felt that the American presence in Iraq ran athwart their national interests. This was exactly the diplomatic opening that Putin had sought, and Russian ministers aligned themselves with Damascus and Tehran in commentaries on the Middle East. For a while, Putin declined to offer more than verbal support. Meanwhile the Bush administration, being keen to promote an agenda of democratization, rejected the idea of rapprochement with Bashar al-Assad, who in 2000 had succeeded his father as Syrian president. By 2005, Russia was challenging American power by writing off Syria's arms supplies debt and supplying Damascus with an up-to-date air defense missile system. The younger Assad ratcheted up the dangers in the region by permitting al-Qaida terrorists to cross into Iraq via Syrian territory and by encouraging a schism between Hamas and the Palestine Liberation Organization in the Gaza Strip. He also assisted

Hezbollah in Lebanon, where in 2006 the Israeli armed forces suffered an unexpected reversal when they attacked Hezbollah's main military base. The pot was being stirred yet again in the Middle East.

Russia's attempt to present itself as favoring Muslim interests was a transparent ploy to tilt against American global power and to restore Russia to a position of worldwide importance. The Middle East was predictably the focus of Russian attention. As his budget came into balance as a result of gas and oil export revenues, Putin no longer had to curry favor with global financial agencies. His criticisms of America and NATO became more severe. The Americans were already losing control over events in Iraq, but in the Kremlin there was a consensus that Washington still aimed to establish its hegemony over the entire region. Russian rulers saw hypocrisy in the Western criticism of their policy in Chechnya and took the view that America and the rest of NATO were motivated mainly by geopolitical and material self-interest. Bush from 2002 had been in discussions to base and build a nuclear missile shield in Poland, Romania, and Turkey. This predictably disconcerted Moscow leaders, who regarded the American project as yet another extension of Washington's ambition to dominate the whole of Europe and gain a platform from which to threaten Russia. Putin could see no prospect of a long-term partnership with America and was determined to assert Russian power abroad.

Simultaneously, Putin strove to deepen Russia's impact in the territories of the former USSR. His actions revealed the character of his basic assumptions. Like Yeltsin before him, he wanted to preempt the potential spread of Muslim fundamentalism. In 2003 his government outlawed Hizb ut-Tahrir. Although his intelligence agencies were working efficiently in Russia, he did not forget about the "near abroad." In 2004 he secured agreement from several other ex-Soviet republics for the establishment of a regional antiterrorist structure. Among its purposes was the physical rendition of suspected terrorists between Russia and neighboring governments.

In May 2005 Putin exploited a political crisis in Uzbekistan to restore Russia to favor after long-ruling President Karimov authorized the violent suppression of street demonstrations in Andijan. Hundreds were killed, thousands wounded. Whereas Western powers castigated Karimov for brutality, Putin sided with him and was delighted when he retaliated against America by closing down the US military base that supplied troops and equipment for action in Afghanistan. Nevertheless, Karimov had long been a volatile actor in international relations. For years he had pivoted his foreign policy now toward America, then toward east Asia, and then again toward Russia. As central Asia's most populous state, Uzbekistan was always going to count heavily in Russian security calculations. Moscow recognized that there would be times when Karimov would drop any desire for friendship with Russia. But Uzbekistan was in the "near abroad" of Russia, not America, and Putin wanted to pull the country into the Russian orbit of influence. He and his ministers had no ambition of physical reconquest. It was much more convenient to find allies in the ex-Soviet republics who would satisfy Russian aspirations for security and commercial benefit without the need for direct imperial control. Putin was following the trails in central Asia and the south Caucasus that Yeltsin had pioneered.

Putin's ambition was always to draw as many ex-Soviet republics as possible into Russia's zone of influence. One of the intended instruments of this purpose was the Eurasian Economic Union, which finally came into operation in 2015. But only Kazakhstan and Kyrgyzstan from central Asia joined Russia, Belarus, and Armenia in this international combination. Having freed themselves from the Russian grip at the end of 1991, the USSR's other former republics were wary of making themselves vulnerable to a renewal of Moscow's domination.

9

Russia's Internal
Politics under Putin

PREDICTIONS OF POPULATION TRENDS INDICATE THAT the Russian Federation will have a rising proportion of Muslim residents over the next few decades. The inflow of labor migrants—perhaps as many as four million Muslims have moved to Russia since the fall of the USSR—is far from being the only factor. Male ethnic Russians, many of whom are plagued by alcohol abuse and poor medical care, have an average life expectancy of only sixty years. Ethnic Russian couples have children at a lower rate than enough to replace themselves—the average is 1.4 babies per couple, and in Moscow it is a mere 1.1. The contrast with Muslims is a sharp one. Muslim couples more than reproduce themselves, at a rate of 2.3 children for each couple. Steadily, Christians are declining in number by 0.6 percent a year, and there is no sign that the process is slowing down, far less that it is being reversed. The birth rate among Muslims varies from ethnic group to group and from place to place. In Moscow, Tatar couples on average have six children—being outmatched by their Chechen and Ingush neighbors, who typically have ten.

Extreme Russian nationalists frequently talk about the threat of the "Islamization" of Russia. Forecasters in Russia and abroad, moreover, have pointed to the rising proportion of conscripts to the armed forces who will be of the Islamic faith or of an ethnicity associated with Islam. The Population Research Institute has posed a set of questions: "Will such a military operate effectively given the fury that many domestic Muslims feel toward the Russian military's tactics in the Muslim region of Chechnya? What if other Muslim regions of Russia—some of which contain huge oil reserves—rebel against Moscow? Will Muslim soldiers fight and kill to keep them part of the Russian motherland?"

In the early 2000s, there was discussion in the Moscow leadership about the possibility of encouraging a "Russian Islam" as an antidote to the perceived long-term menace; this came after the spread of concern about the influence of poorly educated or foreign preachers on Russia's Muslim communities. One of Yeltsin's ex-prime ministers, Sergei Kirienko, who was Putin's emissary to the Volga federal region, advocated a policy of training mullahs who would show respect for the legal order and integrate themselves in Russian public life. Nothing very much followed from this. Kirienko had diagnosed a problem and offered a constructive solution only to find that his was a voice crying in the wilderness. There were just a few signs that Putin aimed to integrate Muslims more fully in society and public life. For instance, in 2005 he appointed Kamil Iskhakov as his plenipotentiary representative to the Far-Eastern Region. Iskhakov is a Tatar who openly professes his Muslim faith—something that had never happened in the Soviet era. Nevertheless, Iskhakov obviously behaves with some discretion and declines to flaunt his religion by visiting the Moscow mosques in the way that Putin and other politicians attend services in the capital's cathedrals.

When he recalled a fire that had burned down his house, Putin attributed his survival to divine intervention and paraded his personal Christian commitment even though he had noticeable difficulty in mouthing the correct words at Russian Orthodox Church services. The clergy pressed the government for formal recognition of "the church of the majority." This was a step too far for Putin, but he followed Yeltsin in ensuring that the Church had a privileged status in practice. The growth of converts to the Islamic faith worried the Patriarch, and he and the Church hierarchy actively opposed Muslim proselytizing activity in areas of dense Russian population. When the Church Assembly (Sobor) formulated its doctrine on other religions, it dealt with the growing rivalry by omitting all reference to Islam. Muslim religious leaders responded with caution. The allocation of public spaces to religious authorities had been a mass phenomenon since the early 1990s, and the Islamic clergy outside the north Caucasus tended to refrain from objecting to the building of Orthodox churches even in the areas of Muslim demographic concentration. Putin himself said less and less about cultural pluralism and vaunted the superiority of Russian nationhood and Orthodox Christianity.

Some of Putin's sharpest critics, including Alexei Navalny, who demanded an end to corruption and authoritarian rule, have advocated a more extreme nationalism than Putin would countenance. One of Navalny's slogans was "Stop Feeding the Caucasus!" Surveys of popular opinion confirm that hostility to the West has become widespread, and it is a mood that seems likely to endure. Although countervailing ideas continued to be expressed by liberal politicians such as Grigori Yavlinski and Boris Nemtsov, most voters pay them little heed.

Putin continued to show respect for Islam—or at least avoided making disrespectful comments about it. The ruling elite regarded religion as crucial for social tranquility. A few groups, notably

Scientology and the Jehovah's Witnesses, were viewed with official suspicion, but Islam was classified with Christianity, Judaism, and Buddhism as one of the country's traditional faiths. Even so, while Putin and his ministers accepted the reality of a multireligious society, the Chechen question inevitably impinged on how the Islamic faith was handled on Russian TV channels. Dismissive comments about followers of the Prophet Muhammad grated upon the Muslim citizens of Russia. Tatarstan's education authorities complained about what they saw as the encouragement of unpleasant stereotypes of Muslims. Their concerns were ignored. Throughout the first decade of this century, television news programs reported about the threat from Chechen and Dagestani Islamist terror groups and about their operations not only in the north Caucasus but also in the rest of the Russian Federation. In October 2002 there was a lengthy terrorist siege at the Nord-Ost Theater in Moscow; in September 2004 terrorists held schoolchildren and their parents captive in Beslan in north Ossetia. The clumsy rescue operations involved hundreds of fatalities. The image of ordinary Muslims suffered from their association with jihadi bombers.

On Putin's behalf, Akhmad Kadyrov continued to impose a severe peace on Chechen towns and villages. Many Chechens saw Kadyrov as the betrayer of his small nation to their inveterate national foe. Chechnya was already notorious for governmental corruption, and discontent mounted. In 2004 Kadyrov was killed by assassins. Intense fighting broke out throughout Chechnya, from which Akhmad's son Ramzan emerged victorious. At the age of thirty he was endorsed by Putin as Chechen president in 2007. The young Kadyrov, with his pet cat that looked like a tiger cub, was as handy with a gun as his father. Arrests, torture, and shootings reduced the republic to an uneasy quiet, and the new president released funds for the construction of more and more mosques. But international human rights agencies accused him of appalling abuses. Brave Russian journalists sought to nail down their stories, and Kadyrov was rumored to have licensed the liquidation of individuals who exposed his activities. Brash and arrogant at home, Kadyrov seldom passed up the chance to offer obsequious praise of Putin.

The overlap between external and internal calculations was broadened in February 2004 when one of the roving units of the Federal Security Service (known by its Russian acronym FSB and feared as the successor to the KGB) carried out the assassination of Zelimkhan Yandarbiev in the Qatari capital of Doha. A veteran jihadi, he had served as acting president of Chechnya in 1996–97. When agreeing to talks with Yeltsin, he had memorably forced him to swap seats because Yandarbiev had resolved to negotiate as if he was the head of an independent state. His zeal for Chechen statehood led him to base himself abroad from 1999 as Chechnya's deputy president and to travel around the Gulf states gathering funds for terrorist activity. As Putin imposed authority over Chechnya by use of the Kadyrovs, Yandarbiev remained a galling threat to order in the Russian Federation. When Russia's government tried to extradite Yandarbiev on grounds of active terrorism and links to al-Qaida, the Qatari authorities repeatedly refused consent. Moscow also pursued Ibn al-Khattab, a Saudi citizen who had enlisted in the Chechen rebel forces and was accused of having organized the 1999 apartment bombings in Moscow. (The charge was false, but undoubtedly Khattab had been prominent in the anti-Russian armed struggle.) The FSB killed him with a poisoned letter in April 2002.

Yandarbiev had also performed diplomatic duties in Muslim countries on behalf of the Chechen insurgents, and Putin and his ministers were agitated about his capacity to obtain the financing that was prolonging the armed struggle in Chechnya. The fact that the United Nations placed Yandarbiev on a list of proscribed terrorists had no effect as Yandarbiev continued his campaign against Russia. The Russian authorities held him responsible for inspiring the violence at the Nord-Ost Theater.

Russia's security agencies hunted for Yandarbiev on his travels in the Gulf states. In February 2004 they succeeded in tracking him to Qatar and killing him with a bomb that was planted in his Land Cruiser as he left a mosque after Friday prayers. Nobody was in any doubt about who was to blame. Three agents of Russian military intelligence were arrested in Doha and accused of planting the explosive. Igor Ivanov, secretary of the Security Council, flew to Doha to remonstrate with the Qatari administration. The Moscow authorities took the precaution of taking two Qatari citizens into custody at Sheremetevo airport who were said to be suspected of connections with the Chechen insurgents. Putin phoned the emir of Qatar to end the matter quietly. One of the Russian agents claimed diplomatic status and was allowed back to Russia; two remained in prison until December 2004, when they were flown to Moscow to serve out life sentences in Russian prisons. The Qatari detainees in Russia were liberated as part of the diplomatic bargain. Putin made it clear that whatever he did in foreign policy, it was always Russian internal security that took precedence. An example had been made of Yandarbiev, who had ridiculed and threatened the Kremlin for many years.

Putin aimed to silence dissidents wherever in the world they lived, and he secured legislation that served his purpose. In March 2006 he appended his signature to a law "on counteracting terrorism" that the Federal Assembly had passed to him. This empowered the armed forces of the Russian Federation to carry out "the suppression of international terrorist activity beyond the frontiers of the territory of the Russian Federation." Such forces could include those controlled by the security agencies. The president received the right to order antiterrorist operations. The new law implicitly provided the FSB and other Russian security agencies with permission to conduct antiterrorist activity not only in Russia but also abroad. Parallel proceedings were undertaken to amend Russian legislation on "extremism," proceedings that gained impetus in June 2006 when Russian diplomat Valeri Titov was fatally wounded in a Baghdad terrorist attack and four of his colleagues were abducted. The Islamist terrorist group that had kidnapped them issued an ultimatum that unless Russia's armed forces were withdrawn from Chechnya and all Muslim prisoners given their freedom, the kidnapped diplomats would be killed. A videotape was released showing one of them being beheaded. All four of them were soon confirmed as having perished.

As feelings of outrage became frenzied in Moscow, Putin announced that he had ordered Russian "special services" to hunt down and "annihilate" the killers. FSB Director Nikolai Patrushev pledged that his agency would "do everything to catch the killers of the diplomats" and would ensure that no terrorist would evade responsibility for crimes committed. TV and radio stations conducted a campaign of support. The legislative amendment of July 2006 was passed in an atmosphere of determination to extirpate terrorism against citizens of the Russian Federation. This reflected a practical awareness that national consensus would best be achieved if there were a legal basis for violent police actions. Official statements accentuated the message that the authorities took matters of security as their supreme obligation.

Not only active terrorists but "extremists" in general were mentioned, and extremism itself was only vaguely defined. The door was left open to outlaw a large swath of opponents of Putin and his administration who had to be eliminated. Terrorism and extremism were frequently mentioned in the same breath by Putin. He was offering a licensing package for nonjudicial killings abroad as well as in Russia. Putin rejected all foreign criticism of his methods. When people challenged him on his attitude to human rights and democracy, he refused to yield an inch. His biting turn of phrase was displayed at a press conference with President George W. Bush in 2006: "I'll be honest with you: we, of course, would not want to have a democracy like [the one] in Iraq." Bush thought this unfair on the infant Iraqi democracy and exclaimed: "Just wait!" Putin refused to budge: "Nobody knows better than us how we can strengthen our own nation. But we know for sure that we cannot strengthen our nation without developing democratic institutions. And this is the path that we'll certainly take; but certainly we will do this by ourselves."

10

The Assertion of
Russian Power
and Status

THE CONSTITUTION BARRED PUTIN FROM STANDING
for a third consecutive term, so he stepped aside for his protégé
Dmitri Medvedev to become president in 2008. This enabled Putin to
return to the hustings and win a fresh presidential election in 2012.
Nuances of difference over policy were noticeable between patron and
protégé during the Medvedev presidency. The discrepancies acquired
a practical importance in international relations when Medvedev
showed a readiness for compromise with the Western powers.

Medvedev was motivated in part by the changes in global affairs
in 2009 when Barack Obama entered the White House. Among
Obama's first steps was the announcement of a "reset" in American
policy on Russia. By stretching out a friendly hand to the Kremlin, the
Washington administration aimed to relieve the tension between the
two countries and find ways to cooperate in solving acute problems

in the Middle East and elsewhere. Obama had won the electoral contest by being the most un-Bush of the contenders for the presidency. He realized his prospectus in several basic aspects. While maintaining his country's political commitment to the American-inspired governments in Afghanistan and Iraq, he conducted a withdrawal of American ground troops. His rationale was that America had already trained and equipped national armies that could fend off attacks on the new democratic structures. He let it be known that the years of automatic military intervention in favor of "regime change" and "nation building" were over. The Iraqis and Afghans, Obama reckoned, were best left alone to deal with their internal affairs, and Medvedev welcomed the change of stance.

The first test of the Russo-American rapprochement took place in 2010–11 when antigovernment disturbances in Tunisia triggered a political earthquake across the Middle East that became known as the Arab Spring. In early 2011, as Libyan leader Gaddafi turned to violent repression of his opponents, the French and British air forces led the enforcement of a no-fly zone for Libyan warplanes, and Obama was prodded into providing support in the form of logistics and intelligence reports. The grounding of Gaddafi's air force was in accordance with a UN Security Council resolution. But bombing raids were also carried out against buildings of the Gaddafi family and of government and police agencies. Putin argued that the NATO powers were yet again trying to secure dominion over previously independent countries. But Medvedev, not Putin, was Russian president at the time, and he had not seen fit to thwart the passage of the UN Security Council resolution. He was also nervous about taking any measure that would result in an overt break with America or even with Saudi Arabia and Israel. Nevertheless, he became troubled by the Libyan events, especially after Gaddafi fell from power in August 2011 and was subsequently captured and killed by insurgents in October. Medvedev began to see the Western military intervention in the same light as Putin and joined him in criticizing American ambitions in the wider Middle East.

The Arab Spring reached Syria in March that year, and within months spread to several regions of the country despite President Bashar al-Assad's measures of repression. Medvedev and Putin agreed about obstructing the moves by Western powers to obtain the UN Security Council's sanction to bring down the Assad administration. The calculation was that if Assad fell, it might set a precedent for foreigners to turn their attention upon Moscow's rulers. Putin, returning to the Russian presidency in mid-2012, made the strategic choice of supporting the Assad administration against rebels who called for Assad's removal and for democratic elections. As the Syrian rebellion gathered strength, Western states supported what they saw as the cause of democracy, denouncing Assad as a tyrant who used imprisonment and torture as a normal method of rule. Russian spokesmen rejected this accusation as naive and likely merely to destabilize both Syria and the surrounding region. They also advocated for the right of states to resolve their internal difficulties without external intervention. The one thing that they objected to above all else was any further intrusion by the NATO powers: Syria, like Russia, was to be treated as a legitimate sovereign state. The Syrian and Iranian governments were delighted at Russia's willingness to act as the diplomatic counterbalance to American power in the Middle East.

Putin's calculations concerning his Middle Eastern policy were based on the premise that "my enemy's enemy is my friend." America opposed the Syrian government; it also supported the Saudi cause even though relations had cooled somewhat when it turned out that most of the 9/11 plotters were Saudi citizens. Another ingredient in the coolness was the growing American ability to use petrochemical fracking technology to supply its own energy requirements. Yet still the Saudi-US linkage held. Putin, by contrast, propped up the creaking Syrian regime of Bashar al-Assad, whom the Saudis were seeking to destroy by subsidizing several Sunni rebel organizations.

Although Assad and his leading ministers are Alawites, who are a tiny minority of the Syrian population and one of Shia Islam's lesser offshoots, they have enjoyed the support of Syria's other Shias and obtained assistance from the Shia government in Iran as well as from Hezbollah, the Shia militia force in neighboring Lebanon (which in turn is subsidized by Tehran). Putin, who was entering a diplomatic entente with Alawite-Shia Syria, Shia Iran, and Shia Hezbollah, boosted the supplies of high-technology military equipment to Damascus. Soon a vicious proxy war was being fought on Syrian soil between Shia Iran and Sunni Saudi Arabia. The Sunni rebels belonged to rival groups of fighters who stretched from avowed democrats to Islamist reactionaries. Assad assiduously exploited the divisions among them. While America talked up the military capacity of groups that it considered to be moderate and democratic, Russia pointed to the surging presence of fundamentalist Islam among the rebels—and Assad warned that if his administration were to fall, the likelihood would be that yet another radical Sunni government would install itself.

Among the Islamists was a barbaric military formation originally known as Islamic State of Iraq and the Levant. It fought its way into eastern Syria and western Iraq and in summer 2014 proclaimed a renewed caliphate. There was circumstantial evidence that Assad deliberately avoided bombing the so-called Islamic State's strongholds. It was entirely credible that Assad calculated that Islamic State's fanatical religiosity and publicized atrocities could change Western opinion in the direction of preferring him as the alternative to "Caliph" Abu Bakr al-Baghdadi.

By the time that Assad recognized the error of his strategy, it was too late to eliminate Islamic State without external assistance. Meanwhile, his air force used chemical weapons against rebel-held cities, sharpening the international protests about civilian casualties.

Whereas Putin spoke up for Assad, Western powers were tempted to intervene to halt the bombing raids. But Obama was reluctant to go beyond economic sanctions and verbal condemnation. Talks to end the Syrian civil war took place in Geneva in 2012, but Putin repeated his observation that the Islamists were edging the democrats out of the ranks of the rebel forces. Despite his low personal opinion of Assad, he treated the defense of the Syrian administration as crucial to the country's stabilization. Obama called for Assad's removal on the grounds of his flagrant abuses of human rights. Moscow responded with questions about why the Western powers were not applying the same standards when judging Saudi Arabia and Bahrain; it also expressed resentment that Western powers were seldom squeamish about seeking better relations with Kazakhstan and the other authoritarian administrations of central Asia and the south Caucasus.

The Russian administration's assertiveness grew in proportion to Obama's desire to avoid getting sucked any further into the Syrian civil war. Obama confined himself to threatening strikes if Assad repeated his use of chemical weapons against rebel forces. Putin presented himself as a man of action while the American administration dithered.

As the time drew near for the Sochi Winter Olympics of January 2014, Russian authorities acted to clear the north Caucasus of Islamist terrorists. There were reports of FSB agents going into Chechen villages and offering a deal to extremists whereby they could travel to the Middle East and join Islamic State. Supposedly, the FSB set up a "green corridor" for them to fly to Turkey and then make their way into Syrian territory—the alliance with Assad was important to Russia, but Russia was more important. Ministers felt little concern about the whereabouts of jihadis as long as they were not operating inside the Russian Federation. In the village of Novosasitli in Dagestan's Khasavurt district, according to the opposition newspaper *Novaya Gazeta*, 1 percent of the population left for Syria from 2011 onward.

The exodus had the active support of Akhyad Abdullaev, who headed the Novosasitli administration: "I know someone who has been at war for fifteen years. He fought in Chechnya, in Palestine, in Afghanistan, in Iraq, and now in Syria. He is surely incapable of living peacefully. If such people go off to war, it's no loss. In our village there is an individual, a negotiator. He, together with the FSB, drew several leaders out of the underground and redirected them abroad on jihad. The underground has been weakened here, and this is good for us. If they want to fight, let them fight, only not here."

The evidence remains inconclusive, but it has the ring of plausibility. The Russians certainly planned to keep their homeland inviolate while hosting the Olympics, and it has been claimed that up to three thousand fighters joined Islamic State as a result. The policy was weighted with obvious risk. When jihadis left Russia, not all of them would die in the Syrian and Iraqi struggles; and there could be no guarantee against many returning to Russian soil after receiving specialist training as terrorists. Perhaps the Russians are merely copying what the Saudis did with their own religious fanatics by facilitating their exodus from the country to join the Afghan mujahidin in the 1980s. Even so, this makes a mockery of poker-faced Russian claims to absolute hostility to Islamic State; it also raises a question about how Putin explained the policy to his protégé Bashar al-Assad, whom Islamic State seeks to destroy. Perhaps the fact that Assad himself was doing little to fight Islamic State made this task not unduly difficult. Any thought that the Russians had a coherent plan is unconvincing: its actions were contradictory in both its internal and external components.

In February 2014, mere weeks after the Olympic skiers and skaters left Sochi, Putin angered world opinion by invading and annexing Crimea from Ukraine. The breach of international law provoked Western economic sanctions. The damage to the budget was serious even before an unpredicted collapse in the global oil price in summer that year. As the economy plummeted like a wounded goose,

Putin warned fellow citizens that it might be years before the financial crisis disappeared. The hope in the West was that the sanctions and a depleted treasury would compel Russia's administration to return to the path of legality. Disappointment was always the likeliest outcome. Militancy in foreign and security policy was one of the ways that Putin had kept his high ratings in Russian opinion polls for many years. The tsars similarly built their prestige on the basis of successful armed power. When Nicholas I lost the Crimean War and Nicholas II the Russo-Japanese War of 1904–06, their standing in public opinion suffered badly. When Khrushchëv had to back down in the Cuban missile crisis of 1962, his days in power were numbered. Putin sensed the need, regardless of the state of the budget, to avoid the appearance of weakness in the way he looked after national interests abroad.

Crimean Tatars who since 1967 had the Politburo's permission to return to their homeland felt under acute threat. Most of them were Muslims, and the new Russian authorities were quick to close down critical Islamic newspapers and websites. Russia's superior forces made resistance suicidal; international analysis of the Crimean annexation all but overlooked the Islamic aspect.

11

The Fateful Years: 2015 to the Present

I N SEPTEMBER 2015, AS THE ASSAD ADMINISTRATION lost several of its cities to the Syrian rebels, Putin decided on direct military intervention. In his opinion, there was no hope for Syria unless the existing administration was sustained in power. While Obama prioritized air support to the Kurdish and Baghdad government forces that lined up against Islamic State, Putin announced a wider range of aims, including the destruction of both Islamic State and other Islamist forces in Syria. As Russia aggrandized its role in the Middle East, it obtained Assad's consent for its navy to develop a base at Tartus on Syria's southern coast and for its air force and signals intelligence agencies to establish facilities farther north at Latakia.

Chief Mufti Tadzhuddin privately urged Putin to solve the Palestine question in the same way that he had dealt with Crimea—by annexing it. Putin laughed, and his spokesman later stressed that Tadzhuddin had been joking. He probably was, but the fact that he thought it a humorous quip tells us something about the tenor of Kremlin life. Tadzhuddin helpfully pronounced a fatwa against Islamic State. Chechen president Kadyrov accused al-Baghdadi of being a CIA agent and described him and his supporters as "devils." Al-Baghdadi reacted by offering a reward of $5 million for anyone who killed Kadyrov. But there were also a few dissenting voices among leading Muslim clerics. Nafigullah Ashirov, co-chairman of the Council of Muftis, spoke out against the Russian military intervention in Syria. The prominent Tatar cleric Rafis Kashapov objected to the Russian invasion of Crimea. For this he was charged with questioning Russia's territorial integrity and sowing seeds of discord among diverse national groups. The contrast in treatment is instructive. Whereas the Putin administration was willing to tolerate a Muslim leader's denunciation of bombing raids in Syria, it treated the rejection of the new borders of Russia itself as requiring punishment. The nearer to home the object of criticism, the swifter the retaliation by a ruling elite that was alert to the possibility that opinion among Russian Muslims might move against the government's policies.

Russian leaders had early grounds for satisfaction. Opinion surveys among the mainly Sunni Muslims of Tatarstan and Dagestan found a large majority in favor of the Russian military intervention in Syria and Iraq despite the fact that the air strikes were hitting Sunni fighters and civilians.

Moscow's TV channels constantly repeated the official claim that the main strategic purpose was to eradicate the threat that Islamic State posed to eastern Syria and the whole of Iraq. But abroad it was reported that most of Russia's air strikes fell not upon Islamic State but rather upon other forces based exclusively in Syria. In reaction to a hot blast of international criticism, the Russian jets for a while resumed their attacks on Islamic State bases. Western powers, too, bombed Islamic State strongholds in support of Kurdish and other local ground forces. Foreign media celebrated the Russian air force's operations, and there was an immediate upsurge in public expressions of respect for Russian foreign policy. Secretary of State John Kerry, grateful for the military collaboration against Islamic State in Syria and Iraq, made a friendly overture to Putin—and American criticism of Russian foreign policy faded for the first time since the annexation of Crimea. Although Western economic sanctions against Russia remained in place, America and Russia were resuming talks. Without exactly saying so, Obama and Kerry valued the Russian air raids for helping to halt Islamic State's territorial expansion at a time when the Americans remained reluctant to reinforce the direct military effort.

The problem for Obama and Kerry was that the Russians quickly reverted to concentrating on their efforts against Assad's other enemies and only rarely targeted Islamic State strongholds. Syrian and Russian planes hit thousands of civilians living in cities such as Aleppo. Obama steadfastly refused to go further than expressing his horror of the carnage and, along with the rest of NATO, declined to demand the imposition of a no-fly zone even though Syria's warplanes were dropping barrel bombs on residential sectors of rebel-held cities. Russian planes attacked the same sectors in accordance with Putin's policy of restoring the Assad administration's authority. Western powers accepted that nothing could be done to stop Putin short of declaring war. The disastrous consequences of the Libyan military intervention of 2011 were also in the minds of most Western politicians: they wrung their hands about the plight of Syrian civilians while resolutely staying out of the conflict.

One NATO state, however, adopted a line of its own. Turkish president Recep Tayyip Erdoğan, a Sunni and an Islamist who won a string of national elections from 2003, had nursed friendly relations with Bashar al-Assad before the Arab Spring. But his attitude changed early in the Syrian civil war, when he announced his desire to cultivate a favorable relationship with whatever government would take the place of Assad's. The Turkish intelligence agencies gave arms and medical facilities to ease the pressure on the Syrian rebels. There were reports that Erdoğan had initially assisted Islamic State. Whereas Assad had gone easy on Islamic State so as to convince the world that he was the preferable alternative in Syria, Erdoğan took up the same approach because Islamic State was fighting Kurdish militias in Syria and Iraq—and as Erdoğan's relations with Turkey's Kurds broke down, he found Islamic State useful in its anti-Kurdish operations. Erdoğan wanted to have a free hand in pursuing the national interest. When in November 2015 a Russian Sukhoi Su-24M bomber strayed briefly into Turkish air space, it was shot down by one of Turkey's F-16 fighter jets. Although the pilot and weapons officer successfully ejected from the stricken plane, a Turkmen unit of anti-Assad rebels killed the pilot as he parachuted to earth.

Putin angrily broke diplomatic ties with Turkey, suspended joint construction contracts, and placed a ban on Russian tourist visits to the country. Mutual recriminations continued until July 2016 when a military coup d'état was attempted against Erdoğan. Within hours, Erdoğan had restored order and arrested the leading plotters and thousands of their alleged accomplices. NATO governments wavered about offering him their support; America refused to extradite Imam Fethullah Gülen, whom Erdoğan accused of masterminding the coup. Putin declared sympathy with Erdoğan in his time of need. In August, Erdoğan flew to Moscow for talks that resulted in a thaw in Russo-Turkish relations and an agreement to avoid trouble in the future.

Erdoğan delighted Russian rulers by sharpening his objections to the Americans. Syria, which had been a Soviet client state until the end of the 1980s, was already back under Russian military patronage; Iran and Russia had never been on warmer terms. Now Turkey, a NATO power, appeared willing to turn its back on its allies and embrace Russia. Putin had attained a special relationship with three countries from the northern tier of Muslim states in the Middle East; only Iraq lay outside its grasp, but this scarcely mattered because Baghdad remained under Tehran's influence at a time when the Iraqi government relied on Iranian financial support. Russian TV channels reported that Putin had stood up for "civilization" at a moment when no other world leaders were willing to get deeply involved. They also stressed that he was acting to protect a legitimate government from violent overthrow. They accentuated Russia's role in the struggle against Muslim terrorism, and Putin boasted that only Moscow was pursuing a consistent policy to eliminate Islamist jihadism. They confirmed that the days of Russian diplomatic humility were over and that America had to get used to taking Russia seriously as a great power.

Putin reasserted his country's interests in Afghanistan, where the Taliban resumed the struggle against the American-supported government of President Ashraf Ghani. After several years of covert talks with Taliban leaders, the Russians expressed a readiness to come to terms with them. This was a drastic reversal of policy. Putin, mounting to a peak of confidence, was motivated by a desire to eliminate America's influence from Afghanistan. He also expressed a readiness to use the Taliban to crush the growing following for Islamic State in Afghan lands. With this in mind, he implied, it was sensible to use jihadis to prevent the rise of ultra-jihadis.

Russia's impact on the Middle East was strengthened in the fall of 2016 at a time when American military activities were distinctly patchy. In August, Russia sent its bombers in raids over the Syrian city of Aleppo as it had done repeatedly earlier in the year. This time the planes set off from the air force facility at Hamedan in Iran. It was the first occasion when Russian forces struck Syrian targets from inside a third country, and was yet another sign of Russia's self-confidence. Russia's insouciance did not go down well in Tehran, where the authorities since 1979 had boasted about the rejection of foreign influence and now objected to serving as a base of convenience for a great power to strut on the world stage. After criticism by the Iranian defense minister, the Russians withdrew their bombers. But the pounding of Aleppo continued from other bases. In October, under severe international criticism for the many civilian casualties, Putin ordered a temporary ceasefire while continuing to argue that Western powers overlooked the fanatical agenda espoused by the Islamist rebel groups in the city. For Putin, the only good Aleppo fundamentalist was a dead one.

During the ceasefire, moreover, he flaunted Russian power by sending the aircraft carrier *Admiral Kuznetsov* through the English Channel and the Straits of Gibraltar on its way to the Syrian coast. The intent was as much to advertise Russia's political determination as to show off her renewed naval technology. In November 2016 the ghastly bombing was resumed by Russian planes acting in concert with the Russia-supplied Syrian air force to obliterate resistance in Aleppo. Housing blocks, hospitals, and water and sewage facilities were systematically attacked.

The American presidential election in the same month resulted in victory for Donald Trump. Throughout the campaign there had been indications that Trump, unlike his Democratic opponent Hillary Clinton, wanted a rapprochement with Putin. He continued to make friendly noises on entering office in January 2017. Meanwhile, Putin convened talks in Astana, Kazakhstan's capital, to negotiate a Syrian peace settlement involving the Assad administration and some of the Syrian rebel forces as well as Russia, Turkey, and Iran. It was a momentous shift in world politics. In every previous crisis in the region, America had been the leading external power. The Soviet Union had meddled during the 1960s and 1970s but never dominated. Now Russia was at the helm of events even though the Astana talks involved noisy disputes. The Moscow media were ecstatic. Initially Trump left Putin to it, indicating that his presidency would produce a sea change in American foreign policy; and Trump himself issued an executive order banning Syrians and citizens of several other troubled countries with Muslim majorities from entering the United States. Putin, who had reviled Obama and Kerry, had reason to hope for an easier relationship with Washington, perhaps in the frame of a working partnership.

But at a time when the Russian political elite were rejoicing in Trump's occupation of the White House, many Americans regarded with consternation the prospect of a softening of policy toward Russia. Some of them, indeed, had called througout the Obama presidency for a harder policy altogether. Trump began to change his stance in April 2017 after allegations by his intelligence agencies about the use of chemical weapons in a Syrian air force bombing raid on rebel-held Idlib province. There were dozens of civilian fatalities, including children. The American administration did not hesitate to blame Bashar Al-Assad for gross infringements of international law and human rights. American cruise missiles were fired in reprisal at one of Syria's main air bases. Washington gave prior warning to Russia so as to avoid the killing of Russian military personnel, but both Assad and Putin's spokesmen condemned the American action as aggression based on faulty intelligence. Secretary of State Rex Tillerson countered by calling upon the Russians to abandon their support for Assad. The Middle East was once again the cockpit for rivalries between Russia and America.

12

Possible Futures

I T I S W I D E L Y A S S U M E D T H A T R U S S I A N F O R E I G N A N D domestic policies operate quite independently of each other. As I have tried to show, this is not the way to make sense of Russia and its Islamic world. Not the least of the reasons is that the manner in which the Kremlin treats its Muslim citizens is inextricably linked to the manner in which it deals with the neighboring Muslim states of the former Soviet Union. Thus, when Putin is affirming his benign intentions toward Muslims in those states, the question arises about how he is dealing with discontent in the Muslim-inhabited territories of the Russian Federation itself. Nothing gives greater cause for concern than the scorched-earth offensive in Chechnya that he ordered in 1999 when still only Yeltsin's prime minister. The ex-Soviet independent states in central Asia, moreover, have their own reasons to distrust the Russian claim to benevolent intentions. Russians and their rulers display something like the postimperial syndrome that affected Britain and France after the Second World War when they gave up their colonies around the world. Russia has increasingly tried to bar the other great powers from acquiring influence in the former

Soviet republics in the south of the old USSR—and it is beyond dispute that Putin's management of ties with them is intertwined with Russian military operations in the Middle East.

Russia's involvement with its Islamic world is shaped by a triangle of factors: the Muslim factor in the Russian Federation, the Muslim factor in the Russian interaction with ex-Soviet central Asia, and the Muslim factor in Russian military and political interventions in the Middle East. None of these factors can be properly understood if it is examined separately from the other two.

In the longer term, and perhaps sooner rather than later, this three-cornered interaction is likely to be at the fulcrum of events as the Russian president, government, and security agencies confront their many challenges. Foreign Muslims have no value for the leadership in Moscow except as a means to an end, and Putin's pose as the Islamic world's best friend is no more than a pose—and a hypocritical one at that. He has no preference about the kind of Islam he finds among his Muslim allies and clients. Iran's Ali Khamenei is a Shia, Syria's Assad an Alawite, Turkey's Erdoğan a Sunni. Russian foreign policy is aimed predominantly at reducing the American impact in those parts of Europe and the Middle East where the USSR used to exert influence. The objective is to restore Russian pride and impact. It is of no concern to Putin that he is raising high the beams of savagery inside and beyond Russia's borders. Putin aims to make the world accept Russia as a great power whose interests require respect, and he tramples on political dissent wherever it arises in the Russian Federation.

Putin's policies bristle with risks. Russian politicians and commanders have intervened in Islamic parts of the world ostensibly with the universal principle of protecting the sovereignty of individual states. This was obviously in flagrant contradiction of their behavior in Crimea and eastern Ukraine. Assad, Khamenei, and Erdoğan are aware that Putin regards them as his pawns in a geopolitical chess game. They themselves hope to use him for their own national purposes. Putin calculates that so long as Russian ground troops are kept to a minimum, there is no danger of an imbroglio such as followed both the 1979 Soviet military intervention in Afghanistan and the America-led invasions of Afghanistan and Iraq after the turn of the millennium. But Middle Eastern politics are more unpredictable than a game of chess because they are conducted without any agreed rules. Military interventions, even ones involving a successful offensive, can result in disastrous complications. Catastrophe has not yet taken place for Putin, but he is no more gifted with the powers of clairvoyance than Leonid Brezhnev was about Afghanistan or George W. Bush about Iraq.

Putin likes to give the impression of being able to do as he likes. The reality, however, is that Russia has no lasting capacity to dictate the terms of its Syrian intervention. The Russian economy has gross weaknesses that arise from its dependence on world petrochemical market prices. The country's international standing rests on the narrow foundation of gas and oil revenues so that the bid for power beyond Russian borders may yet prove to be chimerical. America in particular will have opportunities to complicate Russia's presence in Syria just as the Americans once made trouble for the Soviet Union in the Afghan war. Russia's allies, moreover, are likely to exploit their opportunities to impose their choices on their patron. It is far from inconceivable that Moscow will find itself sucked into Middle Eastern conflicts that its government has failed to foresee.

Even so, Putin's personal popularity remains high among Russians for thumbing his nose at American presidents. He has restored confidence to a people whose morale plummeted in the last decade of the twentieth century along with the standard of living and the value of the ruble. The decade of the 1990s is one that the Russian people seek to forget. Putin has staked his reputation on an ability to continue to make Russia feared and respected abroad. This has placed a premium on the need for assertive behavior; the more that Putin behaves like a mad dog in the global pit, the better the Russian

electorate admires him. There is a growing temptation for him to
take gambles, and it cannot be discounted that he will take one risk
too many in the Middle East, Ukraine, or the Baltic states. Having
played the nationalist card in Russia's politics, he cannot now remove
it from the pack and throw it aside. Any potential successor would
find it difficult to remain in office without continuing the policies of
vigorous nationalism. All this involves a danger to world peace that
is likely to fester and grow.

It would be a mistake, moreover, to assume that Russia's Muslims
will always accept Russian foreign policy in the Middle East and
spurn Islamist criticism of Putin. The attention of Russia's television
news outlets to the Syrian civil war, especially to Russian military
operations, inevitably sharpens public knowledge of the devastation
of cities. Although the broadcast media from 2015 insisted that Russian warplanes attacked only Islamist rebel units, it did not require
much imagination to suspect that thousands of Sunni Muslim civilians were slaughtered. Russia's agenda in the Middle East has the
potential to backfire politically on the Russian government.

The situation is probably even more combustible in ex-Soviet
central Asia, where oppressive kleptocracies have dominated since
communism fell apart. The episodic outbursts of discontent show
that the authoritarian administrations are frailer than they appear.
Local Islamists see opportunities for implanting their ideas among
Muslims who are unhappy about authoritarianism. The potential for
eruptions of popular protest exists in several of the states across Russia's southern borders. One possible result would be the emergence
of an Islamist regime somewhere in the former USSR, a regime that
might well cause trouble for a Russia that since 1991 has supported
anti-Islamists throughout the region. The world may yet witness
seismic disruptions in central Asia and the south Caucasus, where
post-Soviet rulers have kept order by the kind of severities that were
applied by Saddam Hussein in Iraq and by the Assads in Syria. In

such a situation, Russia would be particularly vulnerable to trouble because of its prominence in rendering assistance to anti-Sunni powers in Syria, Iran, and Lebanon. A government of Sunni jihadists in central Asia would hardly aspire to an accommodation with Russia's ruling elite.

Memories are long in Chechnya. The Russian conquest was completed a mere century and a half ago, and many Chechens, like some neighboring peoples, simply refuse to accept their north Caucasus as being part of Russia. Though the latest outbreak of Chechen resistance was crushed in 1999–2000, the tranquility of pacification may not last long. Nor can it be taken for granted that the Volga Tatars and Crimean Tatars will stay quiet forever. Other countries have witnessed a sudden growth of Islamist extremism among their young Muslims, and the Russian Federation is heating a cauldron of resentments.

Both internally and externally, furthermore, Russia has had direct experience of the Islamic world over many centuries since the time of the Golden Horde. It has managed its own Muslims without excessive difficulty since the fifteenth century when Muscovy shook off the Mongol yoke; and as the Russian borders expanded, more and more Muslim communities fell under tsarist dominion. Although revolts were not infrequent, the imperial armies were more than a match for the rebels. By the mid-nineteenth century, however, Russia's pretensions to oversight of the Ottoman Empire's affairs provoked the British and French into military action in Crimea. At the same time, the Russian authorities sought to prevent the Ottomans from appealing over their heads to Russia's Muslims. In the twentieth century the complications of internal and external factors sharpened as the communist revolutionaries tried to integrate Muslim communities in the former Russian Empire while eroding religious belief among them and creating communist parties in the Muslim lands of European imperial powers, including the Middle East. When the USSR itself emerged as a superpower after the Second World War, the Kremlin tried to entice whole Muslim states into its zone of influence even while continuing to obstruct the observance of the Islamic faith inside its own frontiers.

The Islamic faith enjoyed a resurgence in the USSR in the perestroika years, and active resistance to communist authority strengthened. In 1989, the Soviet Army withdrew from Afghanistan under pressure from the mujahidin. Since the fall of communism in 1991, the anti-Russian Islamist militants—unlike jihadis in the nineteenth and early twentieth centuries—have made use of advanced technological facilities. The victories of Russian armed forces in the north Caucasus have fallen short of expunging terrorist groups from Russia's territories. Although the ruling elite has stabilized politics in the Russian Federation, there is no certainty that the stability will be of long duration. This is one of the reasons why Putin puts so much reliance on authoritarian methods to suppress dissent. It is also predominantly why, in a period of economic recession when the government has reduced its welfare budget, he has played to the nationalist gallery in his country.

This has created a precarious conjuncture in Russia, its "near abroad," and the Middle East. The perils of Putin's maneuvers are growing, and it must be hoped that he behaves with prudence in some kind of relationship with the Trump administration. This would objectively be in the Russian national interest. But even if Putin succeeds in keeping Assad in power in Damascus, such an outcome will not bring about a permanent peace across the Middle East—and Russia could suddenly find itself dragged into a military quagmire just as the USSR did in Afghanistan. Should Putin not behave with caution, other powers will inevitably feel the need to restrain him. Even so, talks are preferable to wars; stability is better than volatility. Putin has proved a point by gaining acceptance of Russia as a great power. But it is a power with an Achilles' heel in its economy and with a Chinese neighbor that dwarfs Russia in industrial and technological dynamism. The chances for world peace will ultimately depend on the recognition by Russian rulers that their prospects of lasting success depend on their willingness to treat the West as a partner, not an enemy.

Reagan and Gorbachëv in the late 1980s demonstrated what is achievable if mutual trust can be established. But whereas in the late 1980s the USSR sorely needed a respite from the demands of the arms race, Russia nowadays is looking for ways to shake up the world order. Global politics have entered a time of intense instability, and Islamic factors are exerting a disruptive impact on the search for peace.

FURTHER READING

There is a multitude of works on the themes covered in this book. Readers might find it helpful, as I have done, to turn to the following sources.

Ajami, Fouad. *The Arab Predicament: Arab Political Thought and Practice since 1967.* 2nd ed. Cambridge, UK: Cambridge University Press, 1992.

Allison, Roy. *Russia, the West, and Military Intervention.* Oxford, UK: Oxford University Press, 2013.

Bennigsen, Alexandre, and Chantal Lermercier-Quelquejay. *Islam in the Soviet Union.* London: Pall Mall Press, 1967.

Braithwaite, Rodric. *Afgantsy: The Russians in Afghanistan, 1979–1989.* Oxford, UK: Oxford University Press, 2011.

Bukharaev, Ravil. *Islam in Russia: The Four Seasons.* Richmond, UK: Curzon Press, 1998.

Crews, Robert D. *For Prophet and Tsar: Islam and Empire in Russia and Central Asia.* Cambridge, MA: Harvard University Press, 2006.

Dannreuther, Roland, and Luke March. *Russia and Islam: State, Society and Radicalism.* London: Routledge, 2010.

Hill, Charles. *Trial of a Thousand Years: World Order and Islamism.* Stanford, CA: Hoover Institution Press, 2011.

Hunter, Shireen T. *Islam in Russia: The Politics of Identity and Security.* Armonk, NY: M. E. Sharpe, 2004.

Lieven, Anatol. *Chechnya: Tombstone of Russian Power.* London: Yale University Press, 1998.

Lo, Bobo. *Russia and the New World Disorder.* London: Chatham House, 2015.

Malashenko, Alexey V. *Islam v Rossii: vzglyad iz regionov.* Moscow: Aspekt Press, 2007.

Naumkin, Vitaly V. *Radical Islam in Central Asia.* Lanham, MD: Rowman and Littlefield, 2005.

Nizameddin, Talal. *Putin's New Order in the Middle East.* London: Hurst and Company, 2013.

Pilkington, Hilary, and Galina Yemelianova, eds. *Islam in Post-Soviet Russia: Public and Private Faces.* London: RoutledgeCurzon, 2003.

Rogan, Eugene. *The Arabs: A History.* London: Allen Lane, 2009.

Rogan, Eugene. *The Fall of the Ottomans: The Great War in the Middle East.* London: Allen Lane, 2015.

Ro'i, Yaacov. *Islam in the CIS: A Threat to Stability?* London: Chatham House, 2001.

Ro'i, Yaacov. *Islam in the Soviet Union: From the Second World War to Gorbachev.* New York: Columbia University Press, 2000.

Rumer, Eugene, Dmitri Trenin, and Huasheng Zhao. *Central Asia: Views from Washington, Moscow, and Beijing.* Armonk, NY: M. E. Sharpe, 2007.

Silant'ev, Roman. *Noveishaya istoriya islamskogo soobshchestva.* 2nd ed. Moscow: IKhTIOS, 2006.

Trenin, Dmitri. *The End of Eurasia: Russia on the Border between Geopolitics and Globalization.* Moscow: Carnegie Moscow Center, 2001.

Yemelianova, Galina M. *Russia and Islam: A Historical Survey.* Basingstoke, UK: Palgrave Macmillan, 2002.

Yilmaz, Harun. *National Identities in Soviet Historiography: The Rise of Nations under Stalin.* London: Routledge, 2015.

ABOUT THE AUTHOR

Robert Service, a noted Russian historian and political commentator, is a senior fellow at the Hoover Institution, a fellow of the British Academy, and an emeritus fellow of St Antony's College, Oxford.

HERBERT AND JANE DWIGHT
WORKING GROUP ON
ISLAMISM AND THE
INTERNATIONAL ORDER

ESSAYS published under the auspices of the
HERBERT AND JANE DWIGHT WORKING GROUP
ON ISLAMISM AND THE INTERNATIONAL ORDER

ESSAY SERIES:
THE GREAT UNRAVELING: THE REMAKING OF THE MIDDLE EAST

ESSAYS

INDEX